PAPER · 267

CONTENTS

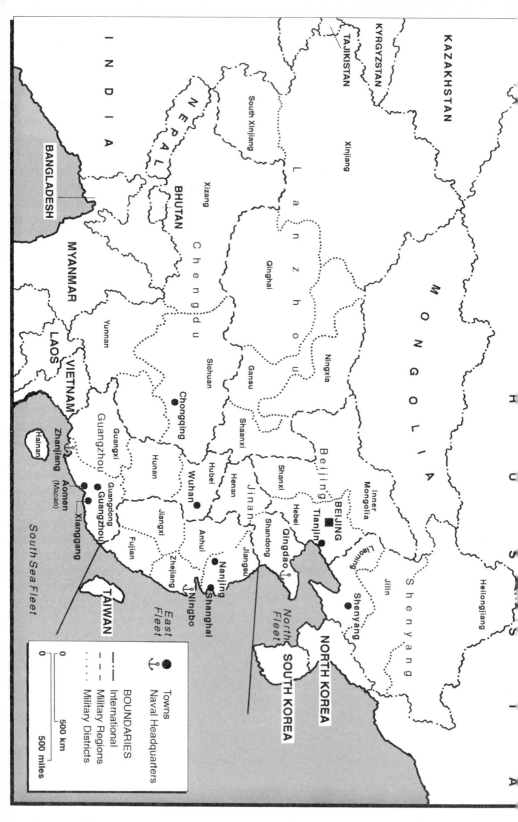

CHINA CHANGES SHAPE: REGIONALISM AND FOREIGN POLICY

INTRODUCTION

China has experienced the world's fastest economic growth for over a decade, a growth made possible by its abandonment of Marxism (although not necessarily of elements of Leninism). It has been suggested that China will have the world's largest economy within a generation. Yet, at the very moment when China looks set to regain its former power, there are growing doubts about precisely what China is.

This crisis of self-definition has many sources. To an important extent it is the continuation of one begun when Western imperialism forced China to open up to the outside world. Now that even the communist 'solution' has been found wanting, China faces a moment of definition created by the failure of past solutions. A more immediate cause of this dilemma is the process of economic reform. This has been based on the decentralisation of economic power, and once power has been devolved, it is very hard to regain. The most immediate cause of China's crisis, however, is the uncertainty surrounding succession politics and the new forces of political liberalism. This internally driven predicament is compounded by challenges from beyond China's frontiers, for even the boundaries of the state are uncertain as it adopts a strategy of greater interdependence with the regional and global economy.

What seems to be emerging now is a less tightly ruled China, and one that is being pulled in different directions by the outside world. Economic decentralisation means that authority passes to different people and groups, some even beyond the borders of the country itself. In some areas of economic policy Beijing can only pretend to rule the provinces, and the provinces only pretend to be ruled by Beijing. In this more decentralised environment, Beijing has less automatic control over the contact the provinces have with the outside world through China's 'open door' policy. Decentralisation has led to numerous fault lines in the structure of authority in China and it is not simply a case of centre confronting province. Although some power resides at the township level and some has been shifted to the provincial level, Beijing retains many important powers. Other levels of authority and

3

influence include the overseas Chinese, China's regional neighbours and even the wider international community. The resulting loss of central authority is already evident in trade and financial relations with the outside world, and is now beginning to affect broader political and even security dimensions.

The main purpose of this paper is to assess the extent of the decentralisation of power and to judge its impact on Chinese foreign relations. While the Chinese government regularly discusses the problems of economic decentralisation at home, it recoils from considering its possible security and foreign-policy implications. When foreigners talk in these wider terms, it evokes memories in China of those who sought to divide and rule the country. The decline of state socialism in China has made the Chinese all the more sensitive to nationalism and localism.[1] Although Deng Xiaoping has often claimed that economic reform (such as decentralisation) can be insulated from political reform, the reality appears to be that sustained and far-reaching economic reform has consequences for both domestic politics and foreign policy. This connection, however delayed, is certainly evident in the modernisation of other countries in East Asia.

This paper neither predicts nor advocates the dissolution of China. Such dramatic dislocation would damage the prosperity of a fifth of mankind, wreck East Asian stability and lead to massive migration. It does argue, however, that it is vital to understand the many changes the decentralisation of power in China engenders, even if they stop well short of the country's break-up. For example, the management of China's economic relations with the outside world, or the Hong Kong problem, have already been altered by the process of decentralisation. In a future crisis over Taiwan, or problems in relations with Japan, it is reasonable to expect different parts of China to have differing interests. As China changes shape, the outside world will need to understand these new realities and adjust to them.

This paper moves from the inside out. The first chapter focuses on internal forces for change and especially the reasons why economic power has been decentralised – what might be termed the 'push' factors. The implications of economic regionalism are made all the greater by uncertainty about leadership and succession in China. Chapter I concludes with an assessment of two other unstable aspects of Chinese unity: the role played by the non-ethnically Chinese nationalities; and links between the Chinese and their ethnic kin in the wider world.

The second chapter focuses on external forces for change – the so-called 'pull' factors. Different parts of China are forming Natural

4

Economic Territories (NETs) that defy provincial and national frontiers and establish more natural links with people outside China. As a result, China's relations with many of its neighbours are being transformed.

The final chapter assesses the changing shape of China and argues that the outside world faces both risks and opportunities in adapting to the new China. But before looking to the future, it is important to begin with a recognition of how the Chinese have struggled in the past to define their identity.

I. INTERNAL FORCES FOR CHANGE

History and culture

Flags can say a great deal about the fabric of a state. The American flag has fifty stars for fifty states, and the European Community's flag has twelve stars around an empty centre. China's flag has five stars – one large one for the Han people and four others representing the Mongol, Manchu, Muslim and Tibetan peoples. The Chinese flag also represents the inherent ambiguity of the nation: on the one hand, the five stars represent the diversity of China, perhaps even a federal China; on the other hand, the dominant Han star represents the 'imagined community' of a unified country. The reality is a China that has only recently made the transition from 'culturalism' to nationalism, a China still remarkably uncertain about its national identity despite a powerful myth of unity and strength. As Lucian Pye has noted, 'China is a civilisation pretending to be a state'.[1]

As with many states, the national essence of China is wrapped up in myths and symbols, all of which obscure different layers of identity.[2] Han Dynasty China and the contemporary Roman Empire were of comparable scope, but the Roman Empire fragmented permanently into numerous states and China did not. For centuries foreign observers have puzzled over what held China together. Some suggested it was an ideographic script that cut across speech communities.[3] Others said it was the country's finite geographic space which led to a relative concentration of people and the invention of bureaucracy to manage what remained, essentially, a series of unconnected communities. It was also suggested that China had a complex hierarchy of commercial centres and marketing communities enhanced by a near-constant technological lead over foreigners. Whether common cultural values followed or accompanied these forces is a matter of major debate. Common ritual was certainly an important unifying force,[4] but equally important was the absence of the liberalising ideas of the Enlightenment which played such an important part in shaping Western European politics, fragmenting the states of the Americas and also played a part in the break-up of the Russian Empire.[5]

An important feature of China's cultural history is undoubtedly the almost dialectical relationship between the Great Tradition – Chinese unity – and the Little Tradition of family and local relations. The importance of family and place of origin remains crucial in establishing status in China. In the past this Little Tradition was as fundamental a part of being Chinese as was the acceptance of features of the Great Tradition, such as the examination system or common rituals.[6]

Because the people of China faced no sustained external challenge, they were relatively free to form their own union, and it was not until Manchu times that the Chinese took care to define their frontiers with any precision.[7] But the absence of threat meant that unity was loose and based on often vague notions of cultural commonalities. At the core was a dominant dialect, Mandarin, but one with six other major dialects and four main subgroups of the one most commonly used. The mutual incomprehension among speakers of Chinese is as great as that between Gaelic and English speakers. Variations in terrain and climate in this vast territory also laid the basis for major differences in diet and 'national character'. China has had well-defined regional stereotypes based on provincial frontiers since at least 1200,[8] and for centuries southerners have been said to be more low-brow, sensual, commercial, individualistic and perhaps even more democratic than northerners. Northerners are still on average five centimetres taller than southerners, and more heavily built. Much has been written about different cultural types in China, often based around major urban centres. One recurring difference is that between coastal dwellers, who interact with the outside world, and more continental Chinese.[9] While it has been politically correct to view these differences as of little importance, in truth the provincial boundaries in core China have been more or less set since the eighth century and follow deeply rooted natural regional boundaries.[10] But the main loyalties in China remained even more local, allowing for what sociologists call 'cellularisation' and what students of Confucianism refer to as the Little Tradition. Community and family loyalties were paramount, and even today this is the thread that links overseas Chinese to their place of origin. China is not necessarily unique in this respect, but the existence of such a tradition lays the foundations for other forces to reshape China.

It was not until the twelfth century that southern China was effectively conquered by Han migration from the north, and the south is now included in what is sometimes called 'core China' (45% of present-day Chinese territory). Manchuria was only really included in the nineteenth century, and the grip on Mongolia, Xinjiang and Tibet is even more recent. The difference between Manchu and Han has been likened to that between jade and snow: both white, but wholly different in nature.[11] While the 'outer empire' of Mongolia, Xinjiang and Tibet comprises 55% of modern-day China's territory, it is home to only some 10% of the national population.

The conception of China as the 'middle kingdom' was always linked to its unstable internal configuration. But because it had no external rivals, and because those that did attack, such as the Mongols, were successfully swallowed up by the Chinese culture, Chinese unity depended on the quality of government at home – hence Mencius' concern with 'stability in unity' depending on a virtuous monarch. The Chinese saw history as cyclical, and even when the empire was rent asunder (the 'Warring States' period) each pretender to the throne claimed power on the basis of his ability to unify the country.[12] China's conception of its role in the world remained complacent largely because it was not surrounded by impressive cultures that might have forced it to compete on others' terms.[13]

By the nineteenth century, when China was acquiring so much territory in the west, the European powers approached and savaged it from the east. The result was a deep trauma. China came to understand that there were other strong civilisations that could not be assimilated into a culturally defined China, and the old order was eventually destroyed by a combination of the forces of the Enlightenment and modernisation. This resulted in both a social revolution and the emergence of nationalism and patriotism to replace vague notions of cultural identity. Urban China was 'decentred', and Chinese nationalism, or what Seton-Watson called 'official nationalism' and Benedict Anderson describes as the formation of an 'imagined community', was in essence created in the shadow of the European (and later Japanese) threat.[14]

Chinese nationalists struggled to make sense of their past, including ethnicity, in order to identify how to meet this external challenge. Even Sun Yatsen, the leader of the 1911 revolution that overthrew the Qing Dynasty, was deeply confused about what constituted the Chinese nation.[15] Some sought solace in federalism, especially as the country seemed to decay into warlordism and foreigners took increasingly large chunks of it. But federalism seemed unable to offer solutions for dealing with external threats, and as these grew in intensity, federalism became less relevant to China's needs.[16] The fact that people from the same cultural zone, most notably the Japanese, were able to pillage China caused the deepest shock and encouraged the Chinese to return to the notion of establishing a strong state in order to cope with a challenge to national unity.[17] In part because of Japan's successes, the old cultural basis of Chinese identity had to be replaced with something more modern.[18]

The warlord period (1916–28) followed the attempt to crush provincial power by ambitious local military leaders claiming the mantle of national leadership.[19] Even though it defeated the warlords, the Guomindang was unable to enforce effective national unity because it failed to deal with the challenges posed by the Enlightenment and modernisation. The challenge of the Enlightenment also eluded the Chinese Communist Party, although it was at least able to offer a socialist solution to the challenge of modernisation. The result was a revolution that, by 1949, had succeeded in laying the basis for a strong and nationally unified state, despite Chairman Mao's earlier musings about the virtues of federalism.[20] When in charge of a central government, Mao would later implement principles of 'democratic centralism' with legendary ruthlessness. Because of the origins of the revolution, which mixed nationalism and socialism, the need to reinforce the myths of national unity were keenly felt. But by attempting to smash much of the old social order (the Little Tradition), it was harder to base the new definition of being Chinese on cultural values. In the end, nationalism with a weaker cultural base would be a weaker nationalism.

During the Communist Party's rule there were phases of relative decentralisation – most notably during the Great Leap Forward of the late 1950s – with such drastic consequences as the death of 25 million people in famine. But once China split with the Soviet Union at around the same time, nationalism was never far removed from the rhetoric of communism. Many of China's border conflicts (with the Soviet Union, Taiwan, India and Vietnam) concerned the defence of what the Chinese Communist Party leadership viewed as its national territory.[21]

After the death of Mao in 1976, a majority of China's leaders recognised that they were not successfully meeting the challenge of modernisation and therefore adopted a programme of far-reaching reforms. But as economic reform raised questions about political reform, the interests of the people and state began to diverge more openly. The resulting sense of alienation, at least among intellectuals, also led to the most far-reaching questioning of the weight of tradition since the 1911 revolution. In essence China's new nationalism was closely tied to other repressive aspects of the ruling system.[22]

The intellectual ferment reached its peak in the summer of 1988 with the screening of a six-part television documentary, *River Elegy*, which denigrated the historic Chinese symbols of the Yellow River and the Great Wall as representing the stultifying traditions of a strong state. The title in effect meant 'mourning for a nation', and placed hope for the future on the Pacific Ocean as the symbol of the 'azure ocean civilisation' of openness and liberalism. In the first part, the principal writer argued that 'the greatest role of an outside enemy is to strike a final blow to a society that has already committed suicide, yet [has] not drawn its last breath'. *River Elegy* was banned in 1989, and copies were literally steamrollered. But the issues raised were fundamental and the challenge to even core symbols of national identity seemed unlikely to fade.[23] As Wang Gungwu has noted, modern Chinese have found the concept of national identity too abstract to provide any serious underpinning for a country facing far-reaching domestic and external challenges.[24] But as the process of de-communisation elsewhere in the world has shown, nationalism or sub-nationalism, however fabricated, does appeal to societies searching for new self-definitions.[25]

Thus, by the 1990s, China had reached a crisis of self-definition. The virtues of strong government were challenged by the decentralisation caused by reform and modernisation, and the virtues of Communist Party rule were challenged by the vicissitudes of succession politics and the gathering forces of political liberalism, chiefly in the urban areas. In effect, the very boundaries of the state were being called into question by the strategy of opening up the Chinese economy and society to the outside world. The external pressure was all the more intense because central government was having more difficulty appealing to the myth of national unity without an identifiable external threat. Being Chinese was now as much 'a quest as a condition'.[26] As *River Elegy* suggested, China seemed to be losing its already suspect and recently forged national identity at a time of major change at home and abroad. Failure to meet these challenges may put in jeopardy the very fabric of the Chinese state.

Economic reform

The World Bank says China is set to become the world's largest economy in 2010, or even 2002 if 'Greater China' is included. Using more realistic purchasing-power parity calculations of gross domestic product (GDP), in early 1994 China already had the world's second largest economy.[27]

Yet, just as China looked set to have the largest GDP, doubts were expressed about the extent to which China should really be seen as a unified economy. Economic growth has been sustained because of the adoption of market reforms, but also because the economy has been radically decentralised and opened up to the world. To borrow the jargon of the European Community (EC), Beijing first adopted 'subsidiarity' as a means to achieve economic growth, and now finds that once power has been transferred to the most logical and efficient level, it is very hard to retrieve. The pattern of subsidiarity is still shifting, but the reality is that the centre has far less control than it once did over the Chinese economy and hence over parts of its political system.

10

Chinese officials talk about the problem of 'duke economies', while noting that at least some of the transfer of power has been voluntary and that the resulting tension can, under certain conditions, be 'creative'.[28] Of course, China's economy has often experienced varying degrees of decentralisation.[29] Even in 1949 Mao said 'we must combine unification and local expediency', while Chen Yun advocated Yugoslav-like decentralisation. But in 1956 Mao noted that 'the relationship between the lower echelons and the higher echelons is like that of a mouse when it sees a cat',[30] and it was agreed that the Party should retain a coordinating role. The fiasco of the Great Leap Forward was in part because Mao's policies undermined the Party's authority. Mao had thought that local initiative could best be tapped by allowing individual villages to build their own back-yard furnaces for steel production, but the result was economic chaos and ultimately mass starvation. During the Cultural Revolution, Mao apparently abandoned his view of the 'whole country as a single chessboard' and instead gave local groups (such as the Red Guards) power to attack what he viewed as a bureaucratised Party. The result was appalling suffering across the nation. But in all these cases the initiative for policy came from Beijing and was sustained by central authorities. Real power remained in the sinews of the Leninist party structure and the armed forces, but powers could (and were) taken back when the centre put its house in order. The key to the process was the centre's ability to act as a single, coherent unit.

The economic reforms introduced in 1978 – the shift from collective to family farming – were also begun by central fiat. They were intended as a better way of unleashing the productive talents of the mass of Chinese who lived in the countryside. But the reforms were so successful and the decentralisation of power so far-reaching that they were highly unlikely to be reversed by another central command.

This is not the place to provide a full analysis of how the decentralisation strategy developed, but a brief sketch is useful. The World Bank noted in 1990 that the strategy of reform and decentralisation was a matter of 'deliberate choice' and thus 'the centre cannot chafe over the loss of fiscal resources'.[31] The centre, however, did not forsee the longer-range implications of its experiments. It never thought it would lose, and be unable to regain, control. It thought that decentralisation would be more efficient and create effective regional specialisation and that the centre would then be able to mediate between regions.

In the first phase of the reforms (1978–84), it was already clear that the centre could not regain control if it continued to allow local levels of government to choose how to spend money on capital development

11

projects. While the centre reigned back its capital spending, it could not control that of the regions. As a result, large state industries were hit hard. The provinces sought to adapt by using protectionism in inter-provincial trade. In the second phase, from 1984–86, the centre declined to adopt real price reform which might have eased some of the problems. It did, however, allow local banks greater freedom in supporting local enterprises, thereby reducing further the centre's control of the money supply. In the first half of 1985, investment in the non-state-plan portion of the economy increased by 87%. Yet more money in the system also led to notorious scandals and corruption.

In the third phase, 1986–88, local autonomy rapidly increased, and in the fourth phase, from 1988, special efforts were made by the new conservative premier, Li Peng, to cool the overheated economy. These included controlling grain supply and price, imposing price ceilings on many goods, and experimenting with a new system of fiscal inspection. To some extent these worked, but unevenly: those regions that grew richer during the decade of reform continued at full speed. The political crisis of May–June 1989 meant that the centre needed to placate the regions, and so the austerity was lifted. But the events of 1988–89 demonstrated that, for all intents and purposes, the decentralisation process had gone beyond anything but the most marginal control by the centre.

This trend is evident when focusing on the most important powers devolved from Beijing. Functional and executive control over the economy and foreign trade shifted from such central ministries as the Ministry of Foreign Trade to provincial, municipal and even county levels. An early feature of this process was the formation of Special Economic Zones (SEZs) in an effort to attract foreign funds. As money poured in, power over economic decisions flowed away from Beijing to local levels of government, local Chinese entrepreneurs as well as overseas Chinese and other foreign investors. Individual firms, some of which were collectives freed from state control, began to make their own deals within China and abroad. As prices were also freed, local enterprises were able to operate according to local market conditions. Bonds and eventually equity were offered in local firms, and foreign investment was earned without going through central government. Provinces set up their own commodity exchanges and central government rapidly lost control of the money supply.[32] The new levels of authority declined to provide basic information about the real economy for fear that the centre would try to retrieve their profits. In sum, central planning gradually lost its importance, and by 1993 only 25% of the economy was covered by the state plan. One of the key measures for the dismantling of Marxist economics and the introduction of market forces was decentralisation.

In the course of these reforms and decentralisation, central government became concerned with supporting aged and inefficient state industry. Local authorities were reluctant to transfer tax revenue to Beijing and hence the running of key areas of the economy was subject to negotiation and compromise between Beijing and various lower levels of government. For example, in the 1990s, the Governor of Shandong province insisted that local authorities must be consulted by Beijing before any attempt was made to implement new taxes. An official in Guangdong province declared that 'our cadres cannot blindly follow Beijing's order', and another was quoted as saying, 'Beijing, Beijing, who has time to listen to Beijing? I've got lots of problems, and Beijing doesn't offer me solutions'.[33] When the central government tried to impose an austerity regime after the inflation of 1988 and the political unrest of 1989, the coastal regions successfully rebuffed it.

As the enormity of the change in the Chinese economic and political system became apparent, conservative forces tried to return to the old system. This was especially evident in the wake of the Beijing massacre in 1989 and the collapse of communism in Europe. Although many observers expected China to back away from economic reforms for fear that it would lead to the collapse of Communist Party rule in China, Deng Xiaoping drew precisely the opposite conclusion. His judgement was that communism failed in Europe because it failed to produce economic prosperity. His solution was to speed up economic reform in order to reinforce the legitimacy of the Chinese Communist Party. But by late 1991 it was clear to Deng that conservative opponents in Beijing were reluctant to follow his logic because of the implications of an increasing clamour for political reform. The Vice-Governor of the Bank of China claimed that the restoration of central power was necessary to avoid 'social and political disintegration of the country'.[34] The fact that the centre (in the shape of Deng) was willing to surrender power to the regions suggests that this was more than a simple power struggle between centre and region.

In order to overcome his conservative opposition, Deng looked to China's coastal regions, where economic reform was flourishing, for support. After initial resistance, he eventually got his way, but the price was even greater reliance on reformers in the regions and an even greater transfer of power to regional leaders. Economic reform, and the legitimacy of the Communist Party, now depended even more on the strategy of decentralising economic power. This was a gamble of enormous proportions.

A major problem for even a reformist central government was the difficulty of maintaining the percentage of tax it took from booming coastal provinces. One report suggested that national tax takings were 100 billion yuan down each year by 1993.[35] But it is also true that central government's expenditure had also fallen, and perhaps even further than central revenue. Nevertheless, borrowing by central authorities did rise sharply in the 1990s, leading Beijing to launch yet another attempt in mid-1993 to gain control of the tax system.[36]

The central government issued new plans at a Party plenum in November 1993, but resistance from wealthy coastal provinces, local governments and rich entrepreneurs remained strong.[37] The World Bank reported that Beijing's revenue had shrunk from 34% of GDP in 1978 to 19% in 1993 and was likely to be halved again if no change of policy was agreed. By 1992 the centre's revenue was 40.3% of the national total, and yet in 1993 the central government's objective was only to increase it modestly to 50%.[38] Beijing recognised that localities 'have different thoughts' on even such a modest change and the reforms that were announced in November 1993 (a consumption tax and a unified corporate tax rate) were the subject of intense centre–local debate. In early 1994, it remained unclear how much power the centre would be able to regain.[39]

Beijing lost control of the money supply because it failed to develop new financial institutions able to exercise macroeconomic controls. It was estimated that by 1993 central government provided less than 30% of the total supply of investment funds in the Chinese economy. Thus Beijing could no longer impose austerity measures on the national economy, and rich provinces could raise funds from local investment and abroad. Local banks were nominally obligated to report to the People's Bank of China, but in reality they exaggerated their spending requirements when requesting funds from Beijing and under-reported locally generated funds.[40] The problems of implementing control are complicated by the fact that part of the speculative capital in China's 'Gold Coast' provinces comes from, and is needed by, corporations owned or controlled by the 'Red Princes' – the children of China's leaders.

If there were any hope of controlling the money supply, it would be by use of market controls rather than by central planning. But as China tapped more into international money markets, China's central bank, like many others in the developed world, learned just how little real control it had under market conditions.[41] The instincts of China's central leaders in June 1993, and even of the supposed reformer Zhu Rongji, were at first to try the old style issuing of orders rather than trusting markets. The result was a predictable sense of 'chaos' in financial markets, and by August 1993 Zhu admitted he could not effectively control the money supply. Beijing sought help from the World Bank in developing a strategy to assert control, but even the outside world's efforts to help Beijing deal with the effects of the centralisation of power were not successful.[42] Beijing announced yet more reforms in the foreign exchange system in January 1994, including the creation of a strong central bank in an attempt to retain a hold on the money supply. This time the basic strategy behind the reforms was the introduction of greater power for market forces, although Beijing still hoped that the central bank could take back some of the powers lost to the regions.

One of the most important consequences of the growing decentralisation was a wider divergence in the stakes that individual provinces held in reform. To some extent the new wealth created along the coastline merely allowed coastal provinces to catch up after a period of excessive central investment in China's hinterland. But by the 1990s the coastal regions were powering ahead and exhibited a decreasing willingness to pay tax to the centre in order to equalise the patterns of growth. In 1991 the gross national product (GNP) per head in Shanghai was 3.5 times the national average, twice the national average in Tianjin and 1.5 times the average in Guangdong.[43] Some 60% of China's poor live in the south-west, and the GNP of western China in general was well below the national average, while Guangdong's annual growth rate was twice the national average.[44] The centre, however, could take some comfort from the fact that not all the growth stemmed from the same causes, and therefore it was not facing a united challenge. Southern coastal regions depended more heavily on externally oriented development, while Jiangsu/Zhejiang relied more on domestic mechanisms.[45] Some hinterland regions, such as Xinjiang, managed to grow at rates well above the national average. But the growing divergence between rich and poor was obviously a serious concern for Beijing, as seen in the fact that Prime Minister Li Peng felt it necessary to deny in January 1994 that such disparities would lead to the shattering of the country.[46]

The question of the energy supply has also been a major economic battleground. In theory the central government sets energy prices and priorities. It is certainly true that Beijing has an important role in investing in power plants, power cables and new sources of energy, but most investments fell within the confines of single provinces and the sale of their products was then subject to manipulation by provincial authorities.[47] The central government manipulated this process to some extent, but as the coastal provinces grew richer, the central government lost control. Guangdong, when faced with a demand for higher energy prices, was able to charter its own tankers and buy oil on the international market in order to demonstrate its independence.[48] This is how the international market economy works, and it suggests that relations between Chinese provinces may be evolving towards something like the pattern of North–South relations in the global economy.

The provinces also sought more power to control other basic levers, such as communications. In an age when foreign broadcasters were able to reach the Chinese market through radio and television, it was clear that it would be much harder to keep those parts of China closest to the sources of such broadcasts from taking greater control of telecommunications policy.[49] Certainly there was a trend towards allowing local broadcasters to take greater control of their own output so long as they also accepted a certain minimum percentage of the product of central television and radio. As a result, local broadcasters began mirroring and shaping local culture, and television viewers in Beijing had a far more staid product than those in Shanghai and especially Guangzhou. The emergence of such 'narrowcasting' in the media helped articulate local priorities and distinctiveness.

Advertising differed radically between one local station and another because it reflected the structure of different economies. Evidence gathered by the World Bank demonstrates that economic reforms have led to a relatively greater increase in interdependence between provinces and the outside world, and a surprising decrease in interprovincial interdependence. As interprovincial trade has declined relative to total retail trade, trade protectionism and the widening of regional price differentials have increased. Internal trade as a percentage of GDP in China's provinces is 22.1%, lower than the EC's 28.3% and lower than the 27.2% among the states of the former Soviet Union (excluding Russia – including Russia the figure is 17.3%). As the World Bank describes it, 'individual provinces are tending to behave like independent countries, with an increase in external [overseas] trade and a relative decline in trade flows with each other'.[50]

The World Bank is clearly worried that as provinces profit from their behaviour 'as separate countries', it will be harder to break down constraints on domestic trade. So long as China's economy remained poorly developed, such localism was of little concern to those worried about the emergence of powerful and protectionist local economies. When there was a strong Communist Party, whatever economic prob-

16

lems emerged could be dealt with by the centre. But as provincial economies grow richer, differentials between coast and hinterland grow wider and the centre grows weaker in the management of relations, the challenge of regionalism grows more potent. If the pattern of trade follows that of the global market economy, this should allow for increasing economic relations between provinces based on notions of trade specialisation. So far this has not transpired, and what can be seen is more rivalry and even dominance by richer provinces which control the production of much sought-after goods.

Central authorities are voicing increasing concerns about the fact that 'the methods of macroscopic regulation and control are neither sound nor efficient . . . the tendency for localities to separate from the central authorities is intensifying. Orders and prohibitions by the central authorities are not enforced'.[51] There is now a pattern of several years' standing whereby local provinces squabble among themselves and with the centre. Products were not being allowed across provincial boundaries and prices were rising in poorer provinces as 'domestic' producers protected local markets. Both Hunan and Jiangxi blocked grain shipments to Guangdong which also increased food prices in richer provinces, but cut the amount of revenue available in poorer provinces. In 1993 Guangdong tried to restrict the numbers of workers from outside the province, but with an estimated 100m Chinese on the move in the early 1990s, it stood little chance of stemming the tide.[52] As banks charge higher rates when dealing with outsiders, some provinces have printed special *de facto* currencies to keep richer provinces from using their greater purchasing power. Richer provinces have used local militias to defend their access to cheap food and raw-material supplies in poorer provinces and the poorer provinces, have tried, and usually failed, to block access. These 'rice wars' and 'silk wars' between provinces have also led to the establishment of inspection stations along rail lines, and Hubei, Jilin and Liaoning have all obstructed imports of food and light industrial goods from other regions. Jilin, Honan, Liaoning and Hubei have regulations permitting only the sale of native beers, wine, laundry detergent, bicycles and televisions. It is not surprising that the Chairman of the State Planning Commission called this 'chaos' and 'regional protectionism'.[53] The central government recognised that its inability to resolve these problems 'impairs the prestige of the Party and the government among the people'.[54]

Central government has tried to encourage various schemes for interprovincial cooperation, but without much success. Various interprovincial trade groups were set up, but Beijing acknowledged it was unable to overcome 'serious protectionism'.[55] Although central government was able to help the process of interprovincial cooperation by, for example, building power plants in Yunnan to serve Guangdong enterprises, these schemes were few and far between.[56] When Henan and Xinjiang signed a deal exchanging technology and services for raw materials, the report sounded much like a First-World state dealing with one from the Third World.[57] The centre also discovered that some of these interprovincial deals were explicitly intended to circumvent central authority: Hunan and Guangzhou officials agreed a deal on marketing Hunanese farm products because Guangdong could offer better prices than Beijing.[58]

For all the complaints about differential rates of growth, it should be kept in mind that even the poorer provinces were growing at healthy rates and national authorities could also take comfort from the fact that China as a whole was growing very fast. In short, while there were problems associated with differential growth rates, no province was suffering in absolute terms.[59] The real pain was more political than economic, for there was a real shift in economic decision-making power to the richer provinces.

One consolation for the centre was that there was no single pattern of centre–province relations. The less common, but nevertheless still potent, problem concerns hinterland provinces which fail to implement reforms directed from the centre. Peasants in Sichuan protested in June 1993 against taxes (and corruption) imposed by local officials. Their grievances were aggravated by a sharply lower increase in income after the boom years of the 1980s. These problems were in part the result of local government spending too much money on local development projects in a vain attempt to match the Gold Coast growth. One crucial error was the attempt to base growth on government intervention rather than market forces, as on the coast. The result of this unrest was decreased authority for local party leaders, and fading respect for the centre which seemed unable to assert control over provincial and local officials.[60] Unrest in Sichuan was only one of several hundred cases reported in 1993, covering heartland provinces such as Guanxi, Guizhou, Jianxi, Hubei, Anhui, Henan and Shaanxi.

The more common challenge to central authority has come from the richer coastal regions. This is most evident in southern China, especially in Guangdong province. With 65m people and GDP growing at nearly 20% per year, Guangdong's economic growth has nearly doubled its share of national GDP to 8.6% since the reforms began in 1978. In 1992 it was China's third largest provincial-level economy and the fifth largest on a per capita basis.[61] In the 1979–91 period, Guangdong accounted for 18.8% of total national overseas investment.

18

By 1991, 28.7% of the provincial budget depended on foreign funding, compared to 5.7% in Jiangsu and 2.4% in Zhejiang where growth rates were not too different. Hong Kong was the source of 81.7% of all foreign investment in 1985–91.[62]

One reason for Guangdong's relative power was its growth rate – twice the national average – its increasing share of China's foreign exchange earnings (some 50% in 1992), and its close relations with the outside world. This allowed the province to rebuff Beijing's attempts to block the establishment of a stock exchange in Shenzhen. The centre wanted to favour Shanghai as the location of the first stock exchange, but Guangdong went ahead a day earlier, with much international publicity, thus demonstrating its growing fiscal independence and Beijing later had to recognise the *fait accompli*.[63]

The establishment of SEZs and open economic areas has also meant that power was devolved well below provincial level. Hainan Island became an independent province and SEZ in 1988. The role of Hong Kong also diluted Guangzhou's power, and Shenzhen was granted provincial-level powers in some sectors of the economy. Thus, while central government's control was seriously reduced, it was not trans-ferred to one single authority, but rather scattered throughout the region.[64]

Reforms in the party's nomenklatura also reflect the complex eco-nomic picture. Apart from the most senior appointments in the prov-ince, decisions were taken locally, rather than in Beijing, by party cadres. Local officials, with their own complex web of personal con-tacts, were far more important for most appointments than connections in Beijing.[65] When differences on economic issues widened, especially as the centre tried to impose a new austerity package in the summer of 1993, there were signs of political disputes with Beijing.[66] Southern Chinese officials have been notably less involved in such political clampdowns, as in 1989, and have been less worried by the political implications of the crisis over Hong Kong in recent years (see below). As observers of other East Asian states have already seen, sustained economic reform leads to the emergence of a 'new rich' middle class and eventually a more liberal political system.[67]

Another, but equally complex, picture is evident when assessing Shanghai's relations with Beijing and neighbouring provinces. Pre-1949, Shanghai was the great cosmopolitan city in Asia and had many 'bourgeois tendencies' to purge before the communists would trust it. Shanghai was useful in the early years as a window on a hostile world and still contained people with experience of international trade, but it also became a hotbed of support for the Gang of Four. In the early years of the post-Mao reforms, Shanghai languished. While it still ranked first in per capita GNP in China, its lead was shrinking. Heavy industry was gradually rusting and it watched with horror as Guangzhou built on contacts with Hong Kong to become a real rival as China's economic capital.

The renaissance of Shanghai has been much touted in recent years, especially since the trauma of 1989, for a number of reasons. For one thing, many of its former leaders have moved into important positions in Beijing, including Party leader (and President) Jiang Zemin and the rising star of the politburo, Zhu Rongji. Shanghai has also been favoured by the likes of Chen Yun as a place that can be used to balance the influence of southern China and is more suitable for direct manipulation by investment from the central government.[68] One official suggested, only partially tongue-in-cheek, that Shanghai's excellent medical facilities, which serve Beijing's elderly leadership, are a good way of manipulating Beijing politics.[69]

It is certainly true that, for all its flamboyance, Shanghai politics seems far more willing to follow the line from Beijing. It sees strength in central power rather than feeling the need to go its own way.[70] Yet there are increasing signs that as Shanghai sees central power waning, it too is exploring new options for more independent policy. As China's cultural capital, it certainly has an intellectual basis for seeking a more independent and leading role.[71] There has been obvious reluctance in Shanghai in 1993 to impose austerity measures, just as the Pudong development zone was beginning to take shape. Perhaps the best way to understand Shanghai is as a melting pot for China, and thus distinct from Beijing as well as from other parts of the country.

It is already evident that much of the new investment is either derived from local sources or serves local markets. This is true of the stock exchange, despite the rhetoric about being a part of national markets. Development plans speak openly of serving the immediate hinterland and eventually the area further up the Yangtze river. Officials note that neighbouring provinces have no choice but to trade with and market goods through Shanghai. Shanghai officials take advantage of the laws allowing foreign investment to be arranged at a provincial level so long as it does not exceed $50m. The centre is apparently often circumvented by dividing projects into two packages that fall below the limit. Local industries are favoured, as in other parts of China, including local airlines, car factories and food production.

Officials admit that they have learned from Guangdong and they too take advantage of local interests that lie between the south and its northern rivals in Dalian, or Tianjin-Beijing. Shanghai officials are confident that their hinterland (up the Yangtze river) is larger than any of its rivals, even though the quality and efficiency of its port does not compare to that of Hong Kong. Like Guangdong, they worry about migration from the poorer provinces, although they value the influx of cheap labour for heavy industry.

There is obviously a wide range of other experiences in different provinces and regions of China.[72] But just because the problems of decentralisation are complex and not yet life-threatening for Chinese unity, it does not mean they are unimportant. Because decentralisation affects so many levels of the economic and political system, it is hard to know what can be done to stop the decay of central power. When these changes take place at a time of major uncertainty about the strength of the central leadership, the risks to Chinese unity grow greater.

Succession, leadership and the PLA

One of the more important reasons for concern over the coherence of China is the certainty that it is about to undergo a major change of leadership. The passing of the revolutionary generation at a time when communism is dying around the world raises the question of whether the communist dynasty in China is finally coming to an end. Under what circumstances could leadership politics in China make regionalism an even bigger problem?

The concern with *fin-de-siècle* politics is reminiscent of China's change of dynasties early this century. Clashes among China's regional military chieftains – labelled 'warlords' by the Japanese in the 1920s – have occurred before when dynasties have changed.[73] The warlords of the 1920s only emerged after the Qing Empire had collapsed and an effort to establish greater provincial autonomy was opposed by local military leaders who tried to seize power in Beijing in the name of national unity. Although the period would later be seen merely as a particularly unpleasant, but short phase brought about by personal rivalries, the roots of the crisis lay deeper in China's social fabric. The epithet 'warlord' only masked signs of deeper trends in the country.

Twentieth-century history, even in the communist period, also demonstrates that a divided central government makes it more possible for regional forces to emerge. Gao Gang, the ruler of China's northeastern region just after the 1949 revolution, was purged largely because of his efforts to take power in the centre, but his power was very distinctly based in a specific and sensitive region. Similarly, power struggles in Beijing during the Cultural Revolution made possible at least one major incident (in Wuhan) when regional military leaders set their own policies. It is true that these two cases are the exceptions that demonstrate the relative tendency to national unity, but the fact that they took place during one of the regular leadership changes in national politics is a cause of concern for those who count on China's centre to hold together after Deng dies.[74]

Even with its revolutionary generation of leaders still in power, China has gone through notoriously unstable periods. Mao was unable to trust any of his annointed successors (Liu Shaoqi, Lin Biao) and Deng has already purged two of his own successors (Hu Yaobang and Zhao Ziyang). Given the longevity of China's leaders, the natural paranoia of Leninist politics and the high premium on personal relations in Confucian politics, perhaps it is not surprising that there are so many problems in handling leadership succession.[75] But the upshot is that as China moves from a revolutionary generation with at least a modicum of unity to a post-revolutionary generation of bureaucrats, the risk of instability is likely to increase. Even the official Chinese press acknowledged the potentially 'disastrous' consequences of a badly managed succession.[76]

There are various circumstances in leadership politics that are likely to make regionalism a wider political problem. The first – almost an inevitable outcome of Deng Xiaoping's death – will be the emergence of less powerful leaders at the centre. Deng's ability to rebound from political adversity and his recently demonstrated skills (in 1989 and 1991) in mobilising provincial support for his struggles in Beijing, stem in large part from his revolutionary experience and contacts. Chinese leaders have some of the longest coat-tails in modern politics, but the cut of Deng's cloth owes a great deal to the fact that he was a major revolutionary leader. Perhaps the one certain thing about the succession to Deng is that no successor will be able to don such a strong mantle of leadership.

The new leaders are allegedly already in place, but then Deng, like Mao before him, has tried before to ensure that this was so, only to find his plans frustrated. The more the aged leader is seen to be losing his grip, and even becoming senile, the more intense the leadership battles become. The *fin-de-siècle* feeling is rooted in a sense of political decay. The result is manifest in part in social decay, as seen in growing corruption or the increasing prominence of secret societies and cult practices. There has been a sharp rise in criminal activities in China, including the use of guns. Some 700 public security and armed police were killed in the first half of 1993 alone and 'outrages' by train robbers and highwaymen are said to be 'rife' (1,200 cases in the first half of 1993 in Yunan, 5,300 in Guangdong, 1,200 in Fujian and 700 in Hainan).[77] This new breakdown in order was partly due to the darker side of capitalism, but government officials feared the resulting social decay and decried 'ultra-egoism, mammonism and hedonism'.[78]

Should a new and stronger leader eventually emerge, some of these features of social decay may fade. But short of another revolution in China, the next step in the succession process is merely one in a longer-term process of decay of a political system that has abandoned its old ideals and basis for legitimacy and is groping for a new power base. While it may be possible to make the transition – much as the Guomindang has done in Taiwan – the task is difficult, especially in a country the size of China. In the short term, the legitimacy of the central government is bound to diminish, and some of the authority lost may be picked up by lower levels of government. Of course, the legitimacy and authority may simply atrophy, much as it did in the 1920s, when provincial government did not fill the gap and the centre was not rebuilt for more than two decades. Conservatives such as President Yang Shangkun are reported to have acknowledged that a 'crisis' is a likely outcome as China sorts out its succession.[79] There is little doubt that these are revolutionary times; the question is how the process will be managed.

A different possible outcome of this leadership politics might simply be the continuation of divisions in an otherwise potentially strong centre. To some extent these divisions currently exist and already provide some of the basis for greater regional autonomy. While Deng had to struggle to impose his form of economic reform on reluctant conservatives in Beijing, he did so by seeking support in the coastal provinces. This suggests both a close-run struggle in Beijing, and Deng's need to support greater decentralisation of power.[80]

The notion of a clean split between conservatives and reformers is again far too simplistic. Some want more reform, but also more Party-controlled social order. There are also forces which would like to see far more radical reform just as there are 'leftist' forces waiting for the collapse of the economic reforms in order to take revenge on the 'new rich'.[81] It would be inaccurate to suggest that the likes of Chen Yun, Deng's chief political rival, are entirely opposed to economic reform or a form of regionalism. Chen and the more cautious reformers know that economic reform is necessary to keep the Party in power, but they hope to keep reform within bounds (the caged-bird theory of reform). They see that the greater dynamism on the coast can be useful when buying legitimacy, but it must also serve the interests of the centre. Hence there is apparently more support among conservatives for features of Shanghai's reforms because it is more dependent on the centre for investment. The 'creative tension' view of Chinese regionalism applies far more to the conservatives' strategy than to that of the more unconstrained reformers.

Perhaps the key to the nature of the succession is held by the People's Liberation Army (PLA). Yet China's armed forces are not necessarily unified, nor will they inevitably play a unifying role if the centre is divided.[82] The military has been a major factor or even an arbiter of past disputes, most notably in 1976 after Mao died and in 1989 when the Beijing protests were suppressed.[83] In both cases the PLA sided with the dominant faction in the civilian centre – the faction that also promised greater prospects for political stability, professionalism and economic reform. While there were important variations in the way different regional commands supported the reformers (southern forces stayed out of the 1989 events), the basic unity of the PLA was retained. This evidence augurs well for a civilian leadership committed to reforms that is able to command relative unity in Beijing.

Armed forces are supposed to be the final guarantor of a state's national security. Yet because the armed forces are also part of the society they are supposed to protect, when the challenge to the authority of the state comes from within, the military is often unable to cope. Nevertheless, there can be little doubt that the PLA is inclined both professionally and ideologically to fight for China's national unity. As the communist ideology has faded, the PLA has slipped easily into adopting more overt nationalism as the dominant ideology.[84] Like most armed forces, patriotism is highly valued as a motivating force. There can be little question that if the PLA were faced with an external threat and a unified civilian leadership at home, the armed forces would remain a coherent guarantor of national unity.

The PLA, like the Soviet armed forces in their day, is unlikely to divide easily into rival units. This is especially so in the central services such as the air force, navy and nuclear forces.[85] Although air-force units, and to some extent naval units, are usually linked to regional military commands, these services all rely on a logistics tail that ensures central control. Access to fuel, spare parts and manufacturing capability is such that no military region has the ability to stand on its own for long. Given time, the Soviet example suggests that many of these problems can be overcome, but, as in the Soviet case, the first instinct is to maintain loyalty to the centre.

The Soviet case also demonstrates the extent to which nuclear weapons remain mainly under central control, although in the case of a break-up of the state their disposition could become uncertain and of the utmost importance. Little is known about China's command and control of nuclear weapons, but it does seem apparent that in certain unlikely circumstances there could be problems along Soviet lines. China has far fewer warheads, but the sparse number of tactical systems are apparently under the control of central forces deployed in individual military regions. Strategic systems on land are to be found in remote parts of China vulnerable to separatist tendencies, but under very strict central control. Nuclear weapons deployed with the navy are supposed to be under central command, but are inevitably deployed with regional naval forces. In short, in the unlikely event of China falling apart, the military commands under central control are likely to remain loyal to the centre for longer than most parts of the Chinese government, but there would be fault lines in the case of a complete collapse of central authority.

Central control also seems to be relatively secure in the seven military-region commands. The top level of commanding officers are beholden to central authorities for their jobs and are rotated regularly in order to keep commanders from 'going native'.[86] The chain of command ensures that only small-scale troop manoeuvres can take place without sanction from Beijing and there is no evidence of these rules being broken in any sustained way. Obviously it is physically possible for troops in the regions to move according to regional commands, but it is unlikely unless there is a break in the chain of command. Nor is there much evidence for supposing that civil and military leaders at the regional level will work together, especially as professionalism in the PLA has helped ensure a greater separation between civil and military in society as a whole.[87]

The Soviet experience suggests that even though the military is likely to remain a centralising institution until the regime collapses, it is equally true that when affected by social change, it can be sufficiently deterred from intervening for the civilian political process to take its course. The incompetence of the abortive coup in the Soviet Union in August 1991 was in part the result of the 'corrupting' influences of social change that rendered the armed forces incapable of unified action. There is a risk in focusing too narrowly on questions of formal command and control in these revolutionary circumstances when what really determines the actions of the armed forces are broader social and economic forces. Even though the PLA is unlikely to fall apart, at least in the first instance, it merely has to be kept on the sidelines in order for a major change to be effected. Deng Xiaoping and Jiang Zemin have both warned about 'unstable' trends in the PLA and the risks they pose for the leadership succession.[88]

Social and economic change has also begun to affect the command and control of the PLA. When Liu Huaqing and Zhang Zhen, vice-chairmen of the Military Affairs Committee and China's most senior military men, warn that many armies have been defeated in the past because they are 'wallowing in luxury and pleasure', it is clear that matters have reached a serious point. They are worried that 'many armies in China and abroad have lost their fighting capacity and been defeated by peace or by themselves'.[89] The cause of this corruption is obvious – the economic reforms in society at large have now infected the PLA.

The result is a challenge to professionalism more pervasive than anything posed by communist ideology, for it appeals to the self-interest of all soldiers. This was evident to some extent in much of the 1980s, but seems to be reaching critical proportions in the 1990s. In the headier days of reform in the early 1990s, vast portions of the PLA were given money-making duties in order to supplement the inadequate defence budget. Leading military men, for example, including the political director of the Guangzhou military region, were promoted because of their ability to earn profits.[90] The armed forces began running major enterprises producing for export and managing some of China's smartest hotels. Officers were among the first players of the fledgling stock markets. The PLA began constructing its own economic development zone in Guangdong in 1993 and another report at the time noted that the air force had established trade relations with more than 30 countries, mainly in aviation maintenance.[91] The PLA began working more closely with provincial and local authorities in order to establish new businesses, some of which took the PLA into major investment in Hong Kong and further afield.[92] Regionalism in the PLA in coastal China began to look more like regionalism in the civilian sector. One motive for this new development was the sense that given the wide social and economic change in society at large, the PLA was losing out and morale was suffering.[93]

Even in Xinjiang, the PLA was urged to concentrate on making money and leading the region's export drive.[94] Although it was impossible to calculate the financial benefits of such enterprises, it was suggested that the PLA earned 30bn yuan in 1992, a sum equivalent to the official defence budget. But the result was also incontrovertible signs of decay in professionalism and the command structure, especially in the richer parts of China where corrupt practices were most widespread in society at large. Guangdong was ranked last in terms of public order, and it was there that the most vivid signs of the PLA engaging in smuggling guns, drugs and stolen goods were evident. One scandal in June 1993 extended to 43 army units and nearly 300 people were involved with at least $500,000-worth of bribes.[95] An incident in February 1993 in a Taiwan-funded enterprise involved PLA troops using force to settle an economic dispute, suggesting the high level of involvement in non-professional tasks. This was only one of several hundred such disputes each year, not all of which ended in the use of force.[96] Although in 1991 it was clearly considered good for the PLA to be involved in money-making ventures, by 1993, as the country debated how to cool down the economy, there were signs of deep concern about how military discipline was being corrupted.[97]

The importance of discipline was vital to those who believed that the PLA could be relied upon to guarantee national unity and the stability of the regime. It was precisely this professional discipline that ensured the army's willingness to fire on its own people in the heart of the capital in 1989. Although there had been some splits in the armed forces in 1989, they were small enough to be overcome using alternative troops (forces from Guangdong were not used).[98] Deng Xiaoping's personal connections with the PLA were obviously critical in ensuring the outcome in 1989, and also in purging Yang Baibing in 1992 when Yang apparently sought to make preparations in the armed forces for Deng's succession before the old man was dead. Given Deng's pivotal role, it is not surprising that PLA and civilian leaders feel nervous as they approach the inevitable succession. Hence the increasingly urgent, and often farcical, campaign to build up Jiang Zemin's credibility with the PLA. When the run-up to the succession takes place at a time of major domestic and external change, the stakes will be even higher. There is already evidence that parts of the PLA have been calling for a harder line against the West in foreign policy,[99] and the Liu and Zhang article in July 1993 indicates just how worried some powerful people have become.

With signs of corruption and division within the PLA, concern over the succession to Deng and the risks of regionalism become more acute. The PLA is no stronger than Chinese society as a whole, at least not in the long term. As power is decentralised in China, it is also decentralised (albeit to a lesser extent) within the PLA. Fear about the role of the PLA increases when one remembers that none of the current likely successors enjoys anything like Deng's support in the military. The events of 1976 and 1989 owed a great deal to revolutionary leaders with strong support all the way down the PLA command structure. In the absence of such strong bonds of loyalty the PLA will not necessarily oppose any particular faction, but it is more likely to sit on the sidelines. As has been seen in the Soviet case in August 1991, even if the only role played by the military were one of abstention, that could change the balance of power among civilian leaders. It would also make possible deeper and more prolonged squabbles that may encourage fissiparous tendencies. As these tendencies deepen, PLA unity is less likely to hold. Even if relative unity does hold, as it did until the very end (and beyond) in the Soviet case, the military may simply become an increasing irrelevance in the struggle for power. China need not descend into military warlordism, for if the armed forces do not become involved in the struggle, the field will be left to civilian warlords.

But the role of civilian regional leaders is difficult to assess for a number of reasons. In the current Chinese political system, regional leaders are really creatures of the centre sent to run the regions. The nomenklatura system is designed to deal with the risks of 'independent kingdoms' by regularly rotating provincial and military leaders and this has been done with remarkable success. Yet, it is only the thinnest layer of top leadership that is regularly shifted. The vast majority of local leaders come from the area and remain in their home region throughout their career. It is true that their promotion still depends on a system that has the interests of the centre at heart, but as coastal regions become richer, the real pay-offs in the form of a better standard of living are increasingly provided by local enterprises and not central coffers. The authority of the central Party system is gradually being eroded by reforms and economic decentralisation.

There are also reasons to be cautious about the centralising function of the Leninist system given how the Soviet Union collapsed. Local party bosses who had appeared remarkably loyal to Moscow sometimes managed to transfer their allegiance to nationalist causes just in time to continue their rule after the collapse of the Union. As the difficulties encountered in shifting the Governor of Guangdong to the centre demonstrate, such strains are also evident in the Chinese case.

In short, there is less reason to fear a decentralisation of power in China if there is more confidence about the state of leadership politics. If the coming succession were just another succession from one generation to another, and not the move away from the authority of a revolutionary generation, there might be more confidence in the authority of the centre holding firm. If politics in the centre were less riven by debates, then the scope for regionalism might be severely reduced.

Nationalities and nationalism
In the eighteenth and nineteenth centuries, as Chinese soldiers and settlers swept across Xinjiang and Mongolia, the Chinese also migrated in large numbers around the Pacific and beyond. But two hundred years later, aspects of this imperialism haunt the Chinese Empire. Among the most important factors threatening to change the shape of modern China is the attitude of both the conquered people, and of those Chinese more integrated with the outside world. Overseas Chinese increasingly see themselves as part of the world outside China, and similarly China's minorities do not see themselves as part of China. The fate of these people provides a sense of the changing limits of the Chinese Empire.

According to official Chinese data there are 56 minority nationalities comprising 8.2% of China's total population scattered over 64.5% of China's total area, mainly in the north-east, north-west and south-west.[100] The main nationalities are some 15m Zhuang in Guangxi, 10m Manchu in Liaoning, 8m Hui in Ningxia, Gansu, 7m Miao in Guizhou and 7m Uygur in Xinjiang. The Uygur are Sunni Muslims and constitute 46% of Xinjiang's population, with smaller percentages of Han (36%), Kazakh (7.7% or about 1m), Hui (4%), Tajiks (2%) and Kyrgyz (1%). Only 19% of Inner Mongolia's population of 21m are minorities (mainly 4m Mongols).[101] In Tibet there are 2.1m Tibetans, or 95% of the population. A similar number of Tibetans live in Sichuan, Qinghai and Yunnan.[102] These three are, strictly speaking, not provinces, but Autonomous Regions. Xinjiang and Tibet have reportedly been classified by the Chinese as 'politically and socially unstable regions', while Inner Mongolia with its larger Han majority has been categorised as somewhat more stable.[103]

The problems of regionalism in these areas are very different from those which exist along China's Gold Coast. This is the regionalism of China's outer empire which has important similarities with the former Soviet Union's nationality problems in Central Asia. The existence of a large Chinese population in Xinjiang is a relatively recent phenomenon: in 1954 only 10% of the population was Chinese, and the total population rose from 5m to 13m in the 30 years after 1954.[104]

There is little doubt, despite the absence of public-opinion-poll data, that the subject nationalities are opposed to Chinese rule. But they are equally likely to hold diverging views on how they would cope should they gain more independence. Tibetans would choose outright independence, while Mongols might choose to control the existing state of Mongolia. The fate of the minorities in Xinjiang is far harder to identify, especially as the neighbouring Central Asian republics of the former Soviet Union have recently gained a precarious independence.

What does seem certain is central government's confidence that its provincial party bosses are unlikely to seek independence. Of the two major features of Chinese strategy, the longest lasting is the attempt to swamp the nationalities with Han Chinese, a persistent Chinese practice as the frontier shifted outwards from core China. This has also long been a cause of tension in relations with the subject population. The second and more recent feature of Chinese strategy has been to win the hearts and minds of the nationalities by demonstrating the economic benefits of being part of China. Recent Chinese comments stress the priority on economic reform to demonstrate that those living on the Chinese side of frontiers are better off than those with 'freedom to starve'.[105]

It is ironic that Beijing is using some of the same economic forces of prosperity (achieved through decentralisation) that cause it so much grief on the Gold Coast. Needless to say there are risks in western China in both raising expectations through economic prosperity, and devolving economic powers that might lead locals to think of greater political devolution. Beijing admits that buying off separatism with economic prosperity is a 'race against time'. Without apparent prosperity, Communist Party rule cannot hold.[106]

Since the collapse of the Soviet Union, Xinjiang has become the frontline for Chinese worries about its outer empire. The disgruntled nationalities in Xinjiang have constantly expressed their dissatisfaction, sometimes violently, and the Chinese security apparatus has always been able to cope. Although there are no prospects of the PLA and the public security forces being unequal to the immediate task, controls have grown harder to maintain in the face of a greater flow of goods and people across the frontier. Chinese government officials, both at the regional and national level, have expressed their concern about 'separatist' and 'splittist' forces, and they foresee the necessity of using force to keep the lid on an ethnic cauldron. Jiang Zemin has stressed that 'nothing is minor' when it comes to ethnic unrest.[107] When people in the new Central Asian states talk of creating an East Turkestan or a Uygur state, Chinese leaders publicly fret.[108] Although there is little sign of major organised separatism, the Chinese settlers live apart from the locals and discrimination is commonplace. Recent reports of oil finds in Xinjiang, as well as long-standing Chinese interest in the natural resources of the region, make it likely that China will deal firmly with separatist forces. Every time there is unrest, as in Qinghai in October 1993, the Chinese can be counted on to issue another bevy of tough statements about quelling opposition.[109]

The occupation of Tibet is more tenuous in the sense that the Chinese have not yet managed to swamp the local population. The appearance of the Dalai Lama in world capitals is also a regular source of annoyance to Beijing, although neither the Tibetan nationalists in exile nor the Chinese government believe that Tibet will gain real independence soon. As in Xinjiang, occasional uprisings by the local population are brutally suppressed. The fact that Tibet is somewhat more in the public glare (if only because of the large flow of foreign tourists through Lhasa) makes Beijing a little more cautious about being as ruthless as it is in Xinjiang.

Since 1989 when events put China's human-rights policy firmly in the spotlight of international publicity, Beijing has tried to stress migration and economic development rather than brute force as a means of controlling Tibet.[110] But the recurrence of popular unrest leads China to worry about 'separatist' forces and their support from outside China.[111] When the Dalai Lama suggests that the Israel–Palestine Liberation Organisation agreement could provide a model for solving the Tibet issue, there is concern in Beijing that it may lose control over Tibet.[112]

In Inner Mongolia, attitudes towards Beijing have varied. When the Soviet Union and China were in direct conflict, Inner Mongolia was on the front line of an important geo-strategic contest and Moscow controlled the notionally independent Mongolia. Now that Mongolia has been freed and is suffering in the transition from socialism, the Mongol minority of Inner Mongolia has little reason to seek unity with independent Mongolia. Under these conditions, China's strategy of giving nationalities a stake in economic reform can be especially useful. But if Mongolia were to achieve economic success, or if Russia should fragment, then China would need to re-adjust its strategy. Chinese officials in 1993 made pointed reference to the 'long process' involved in achieving 'extinction of a nationality'.[113]

Compared to the problems in the west, China has found the overseas Chinese far easier to handle – at least until recently. But now that they are well entrenched in their new homes and becoming more prosperous, they perhaps pose a greater challenge to Beijing. The overseas Chinese are often said to number 55m, but the 6m people of Hong Kong and the 21m people of Taiwan will be discussed in a later chapter because Beijing claims they are part of a single Chinese state. This leaves 28m Chinese, of whom 7.2m live in Indonesia, 5.8m in Thailand, 5.2m in Malaysia, 2m in Singapore (22m in total in South-east Asia), 1.8m in the United States, 0.6m in Canada, 1m in Latin America and 0.5m in Europe.[114] Only in Singapore are they a majority population. Even though they constitute only 4% of the Indonesian population, they are said to own some 70% of the private economy. In Thailand the Chinese make up 8–10% of the population, but are said to control 90% of commercial and manufacturing assets and half the capital of the banks. One conservative estimate in 1990 put the 'GNP' of the overseas Chinese, including Taiwan and Hong Kong, at $450bn, one-quarter greater than that of China. As noted above, the World Bank estimates that Greater China (China plus Hong Kong, Singapore and Taiwan) will have the world's largest economy in 2002. With savings rates of 24–45% of GNP, the overseas Chinese are said to have liquid assets worth $1.5–2 trillion (compared to Japan with more than twice the population, but only $3 trillion).[115]

It was conventional wisdom, as the notion of Greater China suggests, to argue that the overseas Chinese have important loyalties to Beijing, with the massive flow of investment by overseas Chinese (some 80% of total foreign investment in China) supposedly proving the point. Yet as this investment grows, it is increasingly clear that far from bringing the overseas Chinese closer to China, parts of China are growing closer to the overseas Chinese.

As Wang Gungwu has argued, overseas Chinese, even in South-east Asia, have become localised. They no longer see themselves as temporary sojourners and become less Chinese as they trade, work and study with non-Chinese. As they join the middle classes, they live to a lesser degree in their own special neighbourhoods. Like the Jews and their relationship with Israel, there is an important distinction between being Chinese (a private matter) and being close to China. Overseas Chinese (like many Jews) are heavily committed to living and prospering in an interdependent global economy and society, fostering the values of an international education while retaining a particular cultural identity. While the Chinese who left for new frontiers assumed that they would retain a rigid sense of their Chinese identity, they often found, especially when they left for non-contiguous lands, that their Chinese identity became less clear or important.[116] This was the case both because of (relatively) liberal attitudes in North America, and heavy pressure for assimilation in South-east Asia. In all cases the Chinese began assimilating and breaking up along different societal lines like other parts of the host society.

Thus when the overseas Chinese choose to invest in China, they do so for complex reasons. As Chinese speakers, they have advantages in a developing Chinese market. As Chinese by culture, they have loyalties in mainland China, but to very specific parts (home towns) and usually not to authoritarian, let alone communist, bosses. An increasing share of their investment is by multinational corporations owned by overseas Chinese, such as Lippo of Indonesia, CP of Thailand or the Keppel Group of Singapore. The fact that the Indonesian or Thai authorities worry about the outflow of investment suggests just how acclimatised these firms have become in South-east Asia.[117]

This investment is at the forefront of investment in China by the broader global market economy. China gains by obtaining investment and technology, but Beijing loses control because the investment allows regions and localities greater prosperity and power. Beijing also loses because of a demonstration effect from overseas Chinese investment. Much like dealing with the successful newly industrialising countries (see Chapter II), the overseas Chinese demonstrate that there are other ways for Chinese people to do business and that Beijing does not necessarily know best. In essence, investment from the overseas Chinese is more about the Little Tradition of China – the stress on localism – and less about the Great Tradition of a single Chinese people. As Wang Gungwu has suggested, an assessment of China's relations with the overseas Chinese depends on an assessment of lines of authority, and evidence is gathering that Beijing is no longer in charge.[118]

In sum, there are clear signs from inside China that the country is changing shape. In fact, even the official view would not dispute the notion that the reform process has created a number of fundamental challenges to the way it is ruled. Economic reforms are based on a strategy of decentralisation, and there are plenty of official warnings about the risks of unchecked decentralisation. There are also semi-public warnings about the associated process of social decay, especially at a time of uncertainty about the coming succession. There are even doubts about the reliability of the PLA, and Chinese officials also admit the deep and long-term nature of the problems created by unhappy national minorities.

Yet there is disagreement about how dangerous these combined problems might be for the fabric of China. Just as many Chinese are reluctant to admit the fragility of the cultural and historical concept of a unified China, so they are reluctant to admit the extent of the risks being run in the age of reform. But even these far-reaching events in domestic politics are only part of the story. The pressures forcing China to change shape also come from outside.

II. THE NEW INTERDEPENDENCE

Chinese foreign policy has been described as that of a nineteenth century, mercantile power in a twenty-first-century, 'post-modern' region where state sovereignty is a 'Victorian value'. Yet this description is defective both because most states in East Asia still have important features of state sovereignty, and because China is more complex. It is true that East Asia increasingly contains NETs that straddle old sovereign frontiers, including those of China.[1] But East Asia is also burdened with unresolved conflicts over sovereign frontiers and longer-term worries about major shifts in the balance of power.

China and its neighbours share, to varying degrees, an ambivalence about Victorian and post-modern values of international affairs. China's position is all the more complex because its size and the extensive decentralisation of economic decision-making involve it in more NETs than any other state. The result is pulling at the fabric of the country and these 'pull' factors are increasing because the process of interdependence with the outside world is gaining strength. Under ordinary conditions this would be difficult enough to control, but it is complicated by the fact that, in terms of military security, China remains a nineteenth-century power with unsettled territorial claims, willing to use force to settle disputes and re-order the balance of power. Thus China is not only in conflict with the outside world, but at times its own interests conflict. Are the incentives of interdependence stronger than the pressures to pursue irredentist claims or re-order the balance of power? The following chapter identifies how much the pull factors of interdependence affect China's foreign and security policy. To what extent is China's pattern of trade being re-defined by the emergence of more powerful provincial actors in China, and which countries exert the most important pull on the provinces and the country as a whole?

The provinces and the outside world
It makes sense to begin with some basic data on Chinese foreign trade.[2] In the first decade of reform, from 1978, China's foreign trade more than tripled (GNP increased by 2.5 times). In 1993, China's total trade stood at $167bn, up from some $70bn in 1985. In the same year it was ranked tenth among world exporters, and set to become Asia's second largest exporter after Japan. It was also the United States' second largest and the EC's third largest source of imports. Trade as a ratio of GDP roughly doubled to some 10.2% in 1986–90 compared to the

1976–80 period. However, China's dependence on a single trade partner declined from over 50% in the 1951–55 period (the Soviet Union) to some 27% in the 1961–65 period, and then rose to 37% in the 1986–90 period (Hong Kong).[3]

As impressive as this growth undoubtedly is, presenting it in this way misleadingly suggests that such prosperity can be understood as a national phenomenon. As in domestic economic growth, expansion in foreign trade has been very uneven. Brantly Womack has usefully divided Chinese provinces into three broad groups: coastal; border (some can be coastal and border); and inland. The model coastal province is Guangdong, whose exports increased seven-fold between 1978 and 1990, and by that year accounted for 21.9% of total Chinese exports, up from 17.2% in 1987.[4] In 1992 Guangdong's total exports reached $18bn, nearly the same as that of India.[5] Guangdong's dependence on any single trade partner (in this case Hong Kong) was by far the highest in the country (82%). Another coastal (and border) province, Liaoning, accounted for 11% of national exports and also had a relatively high dependency of 47% (with Japan).

A key indicator of the importance of international factors is a province's exports as a percentage of its GDP. There is an almost perfect fit between major exporting provinces and those with a high percentage of exports. Guangdong leads the table with 18%, followed by Shanghai with 13%, Fujian and Liaoning with 12% and Tianjin with 10%. Hainan's figure of 15% is distorted by its small GDP. The general conclusion is that trade is vital to coastal China, but is this trade skewed in any particular way?

Although these coastal provinces ranked top of China's export league (see Table below), they could be divided into two groups, according to the extent of their dependence on a single trade partner. Coastal provinces that are not border provinces tend to have lower rates of dependence on a single trade partner, even though trade remains a very important part of GDP. Shanghai, a coastal province which also accounted for 11% of national exports, had a dependency rate well below the national average (29%). Jiangsu, Zhejiang, Shandong, Beijing, Shanghai and Tianjin ranked below the national average of dependence, while Guangdong, Hainan, Guangxi, Fujian and Hebei topped the dependency league.

The second group of provinces is on China's land borders. Excluding those with coastal frontiers, inland border provinces apparently have only incidental advantages, or else have not made much of the advantages they do have. Patterns are harder to identify in this category. Trade is often less well reported because of smuggling, and

Provincial trading partners 1990 and 1987 in $m

Province	USA 1990	USA (1987)	Hong Kong 1990	Hong Kong (1987)	Japan 1990	Japan (1987)	EC 1990	EC (1987)	Singapore 1990	Singapore (1987)	USSR 1990	USSR (1987)
Beijing	164.28	(127)	289.06	(158)	185.12	(108)	-	(122)	-	(-)	44.24	(-)
Tianjin	227.46	(167)	351.63	(250)	244.93	(218)	-	(200)	-	(37)	62.55	(-)
Hebei	120.00	(110)	341.00	(420)	701.00	(335)	-	(162)	-	(-)	-	(254)
Shanxi	22.55	(9)	147.74	(110)	136.74	(86)	-	(40)	-	(-)	14.81	(-)
Inner Mongolia	12.74	(12)	52.34	(49)	59.41	(37)	24.69*	(50)	-	(307)	98.53	(46)
Liaoning	1,052.00	(610)	471.00	(328)	2,255.00	(1593)	-	(-)	499.00	(-)	-	(-)
Jilin	19.74	(-)	215.23	(88)	180.64	(122)	-	(15)	21.06	(-)	160.86	(134)
Heilongjiang	-	(16)	175.09	(193)	172.09	(135)	-	(20)	-	(-)	358.95	(185)
Shanghai	745.33	(515)	1,029.61	(801)	759.08	(449)	-	(594)	182.11	(-)	-	(369)
Jiangsu	385.44	(221)	653.63	(507)	587.91	(396)	463.12	(336)	-	(-)	110.74	(63)
Zhejiang	226.63	(130)	659.83	(368)	345.19	(203)	-	(160)	-	(77)	94.94	(38)
Anhui	51.00	(39)	177.00	(121)	115.00	(94)	80.00	(68)	-	(-)	94.00	(77)
Fujian	268.00	(61)	1,057.00	(374)	286.00	(144)	-	(60)	56.00	(35)	-	(-)
Jiangxi	-	(22)	208.86	(135)	52.50	(61)	-	(25)	27.24	(-)	40.32	(29)
Shandong	260.00	(130)	590.00	(502)	920.00	(789)	400.00	(339)	-	(-)	207.00	(196)
Henan	49.46	(27)	305.37	(239)	96.30	(89)	107.49	(50)	-	(-)	77.68	(80)
Hubei	61.18	(69)	478.20	(309)	92.56	(109)	-	(40)	-	(-)	83.83	(33)
Hunan	71.55	(56)	558.03	(274)	68.47	(68)	-	(65)	-	(-)	38.77	(69)
Guangdong	403.00	(323)	8,709.00	(3962)	288.00	(154)	-	(-)	140.00	(-)	-	(-)
Guangxi	61.20	(59)	382.41	(263)	55.33	(44)	-	(75)	-	(11)	-	(-)
Hainan	-	(-)	351.80	(-)	32.50	(-)	-	(-)	-	(-)	-	(-)
Sichuan	-	(26)	-	(140)	-	(71)	-	(65)	9.90	(6)	-	(36)
Guizhou	18.94	(13)	43.35	(23)	32.09	(17)	-	(10)	-	(6)	-	(-)
Yunnan	22.12	(24)	96.28	(68)	68.45	(39)	-	(-)	-	(3)	19.12	(28)
Tibet	-	(-)	-	(-)	-	(-)	-	(-)	-	(-)	-	(-)
Shaanxi	27.39	(14)	140.12	(73)	68.92	(53)	29.09	(10)	-	(-)	11.13	(-)
Gansu	14.12	(-)	54.82	(29)	38.31	(29)	-	(31)	3.84	(-)	-	(-)
Qinghai	-	(-)	9.01	(5)	34.48	(13)	-	(5)	-	(-)	6.46	(-)
Ningxia	-	(-)	25.66	(12)	8.74	(8)	-	(22)	-	(-)	4.24	(5)
Xinjiang	13.4	(7)	57.68	(70)	106.05	(78)	-	(-)	-	(-)	72.81	(16)

Source: Womack and Zhao, 'The Many Worlds', for 1990, and Landsberger, *China's Provincial Foreign Trade*, for 1987.
* export to the UK. The export partners data are missing for Sichuan and Tibet.

often depends on the province's level of development and that of its trade partner. Heilongjiang, which ranks twelfth on the league table of exporters (2.2% of national exports in 1990), is similarly ranked on the table of trade dependence (41% on Russia). Neighbouring Jilin accounts for 1.5% of national exports with a trade dependency of 43%. Yunnan, Xinjiang, Inner Mongolia and Tibet are all relatively insignificant as provincial exporters and none have a strikingly high trade dependence.

In short, being an inland border province usually means having obvious trade links across frontiers, but none of these bridges (perhaps apart from Heilongjiang) makes the provinces especially dependent on land neighbours. While these provinces could increase their trade relations across the frontier to improve their relative economic position, they have so far not done so. There are some signs, especially in Xinjiang, Inner Mongolia, Yunnan and Tibet, that trade is growing especially fast across the frontier. This may emerge as a more clear-cut pattern in the coming years. The current result must be mixed feelings in Beijing, for although these provinces remain a greater burden on the state budget, they are less trouble in international affairs because they have not struck up major international trade links like some coastal provinces. Beijing's ambivalence is a major and inherent problem in the debate over decentralisation.

The third group of provinces fills most of the bottom half of the table of provincial exporters. Some, such as Hubei, Henan and Hunan, each have close on 2% of national exports. Anhui, Jiangxi, Shaanxi and Shanxi each have close on 1%, while Gansu, Guizhou, Ningxia and Qinghai bring up the rear. Most of these provinces have trade dependencies above the national average. The most striking cases are Qinghai (54% on Japan), Hunan (47% on Hong Kong), Hubei (47% on Hong Kong) and Shanxi (45% on Hong Kong), appearing in the top ten provinces ranked according to trade dependence.

Since none of these provinces is close to its main export markets, it is hard to see a relationship of real dependence. Only in Hunan, where relatively high levels of dependence and provincial exports coincide, can it be argued that trade is important, but the dependence seems to be a secondary effect of Guangdong's dependence on Hong Kong. This argues in favour of looking more at regional patterns of dependence on the outside world than just on provincial boundaries.

Further evidence of this complexity comes from David Zweig, who argues that the role of township enterprises is rising so sharply – 20% of total national exports in 1991 – that certain townships, especially in border provinces, have developed particularly heavy dependence on foreign trade.[6] To complicate matters further, these townships and village enterprises also power the growth of such provinces as Jiangsu and Zhejiang where dependence on foreign trade is not nearly as high as it is in southern China.[7] There are some 19 border towns in Heilongjiang facing Russia that have mean growth rates well above the national average because of trade across the frontiers.[8] Therefore the argument can be widened to show the danger of looking too closely at the provincial level of trade when the process often focuses on areas smaller or larger than the province.[9]

One basic pattern which does emerge is a limited, but nevertheless still important form of dependence linking some regions of China with the outside world. The two obvious regions are southern China linking Guangdong, Fujian, Hainan and neighbouring hinterland provinces with Hong Kong and Taiwan; and a northern coastal region focused on Liaoning which links with Japan. Less clear evidence suggests that Shandong can be linked to this second region, or else has a special connection with South Korea. Another possibility is Heilongjiang and perhaps Jilin becoming more tied to Russia, or Guangxi and Yunnan connecting with Vietnam and Myanmar. But like other inland border regions, there is scope for far more regional connections across frontiers before the NETs can begin to emerge as really important features.

From Beijing's point of view, the pattern of NETs is still manageable. Only two NETs are powerful and because China as a whole benefits from close relations with Hong Kong, Taiwan and Japan, the effect can be diffused, especially as overseas finance seeks cheaper labour further inland. Yet it is also clear that the opening up of the provinces to foreign trade, based as it is on 'market localism', has great potential to develop according to market forces and outside central control. Market specialisation has replaced the Maoist ideal of self-sufficiency and material incentives have spurred local initiative.[10] As provinces and regions diversify and grow they will be more difficult to handle. One can already begin to conceive of several provinces as independent trading powers. The logical outcome should be greater diversification of production and more complex trade relations between provinces. The provinces will also be less inclined to need Beijing's services and more likely to resent its interference. If interprovincial relations become more akin to North–South relations in the international system, Beijing may be called upon to be more involved in settling trade disputes.

Beijing also derives strength from the fact that China is seeking wider membership in, and contacts with, international economic institutions. Although these institutions, such as the IMF and World Bank, do have teams working in different parts of China, central government has retained basic control of the relationship. Chinese membership in the General Agreement on Tariffs and Trade (GATT) is especially desired by Beijing because if membership requires the regions to provide more reporting of data, then the centre will gain power over otherwise freer enterprise in coastal regions. The same transparency that GATT requires of China as a whole will be required by Beijing of its provinces. Indeed, Beijing and international institutions often share common interests. The most egregious cases of Chinese enterprises receiving GATT-violating subsidies or flouting intellectual property rules are to be found at the provincial or township and village enterprise level.[11] Beijing may want to abide by international agreements on these matters, but it simply does not control that part of the economy.

While the functioning of the NETs is made possible by the growing autonomy of certain provinces, it is also dependent on specific policies of China's neighbours. But these neighbours are not only concerned with the economic basis of the relationship with parts of China, they are also concerned with security issues. One of many complications in the operations of these NETs is that while economic relations are increasingly localised in specific parts of China, security issues still concern Beijing and not the provinces.

Hong Kong

By far the tightest NET is that which links Hong Kong to Guangdong province and includes virtually all of southern China. Within this NET are unusual security issues concerning the fate of Hong Kong.[12] On 1 July 1997 Hong Kong will become part of China, and what were once considered external relations will become a special sort of internal affairs. It is not surprising that the decade or so since the 1984 Anglo-Chinese accord on Hong Kong has been taken up with managing the convergence of the colony and China.

Conventional wisdom suggested that China would take increasing charge of convergence as 1997 approached. But the Hong Kong problem has been far more complex. In fact southern China (and especially Guangdong) is changing faster than Hong Kong on its way to convergence with the British colony. This process both pulls southern China further away from Beijing and strengthens the hand of foreigners who operate in and through Hong Kong. The extent to which Beijing has lost control of this process is evident in the way in which the Chinese trade surplus with the United States has grown into a major problem in Sino-American relations, even though it is largely due to the transfer of a large part of Hong Kong's (and Taiwan's) trade surplus to production within China. As the United States threatened China with restrictions on exports and thereby forced concessions on trade and human-rights policy, most of this American power was made available by decisions taken in Hong Kong and Taiwan.

The power of Hong Kong also derives from the fact that it is essential to the growth of southern China, and growth in southern China is essential for the growth of the country at large. Without this growth, the legitimacy of the Communist Party in Beijing is at risk.

The close connection between Hong Kong and southern China is evident in a number of ways. Most important is the undoubted dependence of Guangdong on Hong Kong for investment and trade. Some 75% of total Guangdong exports pass through Hong Kong, and the British colony employs some 3m people in the Chinese province. In 1990, some 55% of Hong Kong's massive imports from China came from Guangdong and Fujian. Hong Kong was by far the most important trade partner for all of China, and most Chinese provinces had Hong Kong as their main export market. In 1992, 44% of Chinese exports and 25% of its imports passed through Hong Kong, up from 26% and 12% respectively in 1984. Hong Kong and Macao accounted for 70% of all direct investment in China in 1992, up from 52% in 1984. In 1990 the colony accounted for 37% of all provincial exports, up from 30% in 1987. But the volume of trade and investment flows remained heavily weighted towards southern China.[13]

The cross-border connections also include ties between local gangsters and a flourishing narcotics trade.[14] By 1993 the problems had grown so serious that the PLA navy was called in to deal with anti-smuggling operations. But the navy itself had been so corrupted by the vast amounts of money to be made in southern China that it proved ineffective in stopping the smuggling.[15] The problem at sea is in fact part of a wider one that China is experiencing since provinces were given responsibility for managing territorial waters in 1992.[16] Piracy has become a more prominent problem in the 1990s, in part because it is related to the booming drug and gun running in Guangxi province. Criminal gangs in Fujian are key players in the smuggling of Chinese into the United States, thus helping to create wider international problems.[17] Thus, as even the reliability of the PLA was being called into question, there could be no doubt that Hong Kong was having a major impact on Chinese foreign policy and, from Beijing's perspective, often a deleterious impact.

Cross-border links are also well grounded in close ethnic and family ties and are fuelled daily by the tens of thousands of people who cross the frontier for work and social reasons. Some 30% of Hong Kong dollar notes circulate in southern China.[18] Some 21% of Guangdong's industrial output is generated by joint ventures and foreign-owned enterprises (the national total is 4%), and Guangdong's foreign enterprises account for some 37% of the industrial output of all such enterprises in China. Over 75% of realised foreign direct investment in Guangdong comes from Hong Kong, and 57% of total foreign investment in China in 1979–92 came from Hong Kong.[19]

As the NET connecting Hong Kong and southern China grows tighter because of explicit Hong Kong and Chinese policy, the implications extend well beyond the economic prosperity of the region. The wider political and security implications derive primarily from the fact that the fate of Hong Kong is part of the wider issue of how China manages national reunification. The intensified row between London and Beijing over Hong Kong has demonstrated the extent to which Britain's (and Hong Kong's) hand is strengthened by the convergence of Hong Kong and southern China. When Beijing tried to shake confidence in the colony in 1992–93 to undermine support for Governor Chris Patten, it was investment from southern China into the Hong Kong stock market in early 1993 that buoyed up confidence in the colony and undermined Beijing. The mixture of flight capital from China and sound investment decisions by Chinese firms have made Hong Kong a net importer of capital from China since 1992. As Hong Kong grows more important to the prosperity of southern China, Chinese officials have grown increasingly worried that Britain and Hong Kong are deliberately using their new economic power to improve their bargaining on the colony's political fate. China's recent concern that Britain sees Hong Kong not just as an economic centre, but also as a political entity, with demands of its own, is a vivid case in point.[20]

The best explanation for recent events is that as Hong Kong and China have converged, contrary to Beijing's initial expectation, central government has lost some control over how the Hong Kong issue is resolved. As a result, Beijing is also less in control of how the wider issue of national reunification is managed. When it failed to force Britain to withdraw its proposals for greater democratisation, Beijing set in motion plans to set up an alternative structure of government for Hong Kong. Beijing hoped that it, rather than the southern Chinese, would run Hong Kong after 1997, although the outcome of that power struggle will only be known after the British withdraw. By acting as the service hub for the southern Chinese economy, Hong Kong is trying to ensure that it has a closer relationship with Guangdong and that after 1997 their combined forces will be better able to resist

Beijing. So long as growth in the coastal regions remains essential to the strategy that keeps the Communist Party in power in Beijing, Hong Kong will continue to exert important leverage over policies in Beijing. The NET that includes Hong Kong is obviously the tightest and most important on China's periphery, and its strength demonstrates the extent to which China's foreign policy is altered by domestic decentralisation and international interdependence.

Taiwan

One reason why the relationship with Hong Kong is so sensitive, and the loss of power by Beijing so significant, is that more is at stake than just the fate of Hong Kong. The fate of the 21m people of Taiwan is also bound up with this issue. In fact, it is far more accurate to talk of a southern Chinese NET, where Hong Kong and Taiwan are joined with Guangdong, Fujian and Hainan into an increasingly tight economic unit. Taiwan once had a particular interest in strengthening ties with Fujian across the straits, but what has evolved is a wider NET in southern China.[21]

Data on trade are scarce and unreliable, if only because until recently most of Taiwan's trade with China passed through Hong Kong. Recent estimates suggest that Taiwanese investment in China in 1992 was $5.5bn, over and above the cumulative investment of $3.4bn in the previous decade.[22] By April 1993 there were reportedly some 12,000 Taiwanese-funded enterprises in China. Two-way trade in 1992 stood at some $7bn, and was up 25% in 1993.[23] About 1.5m Taiwanese visited the mainland in 1992, triple the figure in 1989, and nearly 30m phone calls were made to China in 1992, an increase from less than 10m in 1990.[24] Data on the extent of concentration of these links in southern China are not reliable, but anecdotal evidence points to the conclusion that, as in the case of Hong Kong, investment is present in impressive totals around the country, but the heaviest concentration is in the southern Chinese NET. As Taiwanese investment in Shanghai grows rapidly, Taiwanese firms speak of developing separate regional strategies for investment.[25]

The fact that Taiwan and China held their first high-level talks in Singapore in April 1993 indicates the extent to which economic convergence has caused changes in the political relationship. The selection of the predominantly ethnic Chinese city-state of Singapore worried those who feared the power of Greater China. But it is clear that China does not have commanding authority over a wider, ethnically based community. Unlike Hong Kong, Taiwan is not necessarily destined to accept unity on China's terms. As Taiwan has grown richer, its emerging middle class has changed the political system, with a resulting increase in support for political parties favouring greater independence. The more Taiwan is able to operate as a normal international actor, the less it will feel the need to surrender its *de facto* independence. Taiwan's trade with China has several advantages for Taipei. Not only does it bring economic benefits, but it makes it harder for third parties to refuse decent relations with Taiwan if China is prepared to be pragmatic. Because the trade is so heavily focused on southern China, like that of Hong Kong, the result is a more powerful southern Chinese NET able to resist the will of Beijing.

Taiwan's encouragement of regional autonomy, at least in trade, gives it a role different from that of Hong Kong. The greater the autonomy given to China's provinces, the more *de facto* independence for Taiwan is made plausible. Economic interdependence buys greater political independence. Taiwan's wealth and its ability to resist pressure from Beijing are connected, and offer a model of sorts to China's own more independently minded provinces. Greater China means closer economic relations with the mainland, but greater political fragmentation of China in its widest sense.

In part because of the growing worries about the basis of social order in China, Hong Kong and Taiwan, investors have been ensuring that their investment is not too heavily concentrated in southern China. Jiangsu province has been especially assiduous in courting Taiwanese investment and by mid-1993 had 423 enterprises with a total investment value of $768m.[26] By giving a wider area of China a stake in seeking investment from Hong Kong and Taiwan, other regions can be strengthened in competition with southern China. By bargaining with different provinces, investors risk Beijing's ire, but in general Beijing will welcome such a trend if it makes managing the most powerful NET in southern China easier. Yet such an ability to fine-tune investment for strategic reasons is unlikely. Money is invested for a mixture of good business reasons and cultural factors and is therefore most likely to remain concentrated in southern China. But if such concentration and convergence is sustained in the southern Chinese NET, there are major implications for Beijing's ability to maintain China's unity. Short of a looser, informally federal structure, market and political forces are likely to pull southern China further from Beijing's grasp. As this process gathers pace, Beijing may well find that its richer coastal regions are reluctant to risk their prosperity for the sake of a forced reunification with Taiwan.

South-east Asia

The role of the overseas Chinese demonstrates that the 'pulling' on the fabric of China that comes from Hong Kong and Taiwan is also part of a process involving the wider Chinese world. Most of the overseas Chinese who do not live in Hong Kong and Taiwan live in South-east Asia, and their presence is only one of a number of reasons for the region's distinctive approach to China and its unity.

China is becoming an increasingly important trade partner for many states in South-east Asia, but its relationships are many and varied. There is the case of Mandarin-speaking Singapore which, despite cultural connections to southern China, is trying very hard to operate throughout China. Total Singapore trade with China is the largest among South-east Asian states. In 1991 its $3bn of total trade was 37% of South-east Asia's total trade with China. China's exports to Singapore were nearly 3% of China's total. In 1979–91 total Singapore investment in China was $897m, but in 1992 alone it was $997m. Provincial exports from China in 1990 were only 1.8%, up from 1.2% in 1987, but still low enough to suggest that Singapore was notable for focusing on trade with national rather than provincial enterprises. A recent Singapore investment scheme concerns plans to invest some $20bn in a township in Suzhou near Shanghai. The initiative came from Beijing which wanted to encourage the creation of another model of development involving overseas Chinese not tied to Hong Kong or Taiwan.[27] But Lee Kuan Yew also took a delegation to Shandong and, by his own admission, implicitly suggested that Singapore was bargaining over terms of investment by playing off Shandong, Suzhou and other provinces anxious for investment.[28]

Singapore is, ethnically, mainly a Chinese state and its impressive trade links with China can be explained by the strong trading advantages that overseas Chinese have in the China market. Given the distance between Singapore and the Chinese coast, it is clear that Singapore's economic relations are not tied up with questions of national reunification. But Lee Kuan Yew has seen himself as an elder statesman of the overseas Chinese and a voice in the debate about China's role in the world. He has argued against those in the West who would press China on human rights and trade issues, and has urged quiet diplomacy in order to make China a more cooperative player in East Asian affairs. Such a line of argument endears him to Beijing, but garners little support outside the ethnic Chinese world. In fact, Lee's approach raises suspicions about the powers and intentions of China and overseas Chinese. While the overseas Chinese as a business community help pull coastal China further out into the world of interna-

44

tional interdependence, Lee Kuan Yew is seen to be strengthening Chinese nationalism and in effect souring relations in South-east Asia, especially among those who worry about China's irredentist agenda.

South-east Asians are unsure whether China is a threat, and if so, what kind of threat precisely. One way that China copes with its concern over the impact of its reforms is to take a tough line on nationalist issues – hence Beijing's active and vigorous pursuit of claims in the South China Sea. Leaving aside the question of whether China's claim is stronger than others, the regular use of force in seizing islands demonstrates that nationalism comes before a cautious calculation of the impact on regional trade relations. Surely it makes no economic sense for China to continue to scare South-east Asians and the wider international community with its determination to regain lost territory? It only makes sense if China feels that its neighbours and the rest of the world need to learn that China will be ruthless in taking what it claims to be rightfully its own. China's strategy is nationalist and constrained only by the limits on its military power and potential political costs.[29] Energy supplies and other resources are set to become even more vital to a growing Chinese economy, and China would rather control these by itself than be required to trade with others. Military officials in China are thus quick to make the geo-economic case for the use of force.

The use of force in the South China Sea has apparently been determined by the leadership in Beijing and, unlike the case of Hong Kong, there are not yet any clear signs of regional opposition to a hard, nationalist policy.[30] Yet it is not impossible to imagine situations in which regional leaders object to actions ordered by the centre that could damage them economically.

There is also evidence that China's agenda is not just nationalist in the sense of regaining lost territory, but also in the sense of demonstrating dominance in the region. China's systematic humiliation of Vietnam, even in the years following Hanoi's withdrawal from Cambodia and normalisation of relations with China, is a case in point.[31] The problem is that China defines 'normal' relations with Vietnam as ones where Vietnam is subservient to China. Even the growing cross-border trade relations between Chinese and Vietnamese provinces follow a pattern of Chinese domination.[32]

The unique problems of Yunnan and Guangxi indicate where the Chinese can lose some control of policy towards South-east Asia. Drug and gun running are rapidly increasingly, and the problem is beyond the control of central and provincial government. Some villages even straddle the frontier. The commerce is part of a 'black NET' linking these provinces with Vietnam, Myanmar and Thailand. Narcotics use is also on the increase throughout China and the inability to block supply routes is part of the reason. Hong Kong is also involved in the drug and gun trade. These problems contribute to social decay and make the maintenance of order, especially in major cities, more difficult.[33]

Although Thailand and Myanmar are most concerned with managing the drug trade, the rest of South-east Asia is also anxious to control the problem. Whether the trade is in drugs and guns or other less unpleasant products, China has a large trade surplus with its southern neighbours. Vietnam tried to deal with the problem by raising import tariffs in October 1993, but as most of the trade was illegal anyway, the measures were expected to have little impact.[34]

The wider question for many South-east Asians is whether China is better placated or deterred. Vietnam, Malaysia, Indonesia, the Philippines and perhaps even Thailand have good reason to seek early answers. A China that is aware of its vulnerabilities when contemplating the agenda for economic interdependence, and yet free to use force in the region as it sees fit, will want to use such power as it has to tip the balance of advantage its way. Japanese economic investments in South-east Asia seem to have already passed their peak, and in any case could never be an effective counter to either fully developed Chinese economic or military power. Without a balance of power, South-east Asians are vulnerable.

Arguments that increasing economic interdependence will keep China from using force are simply not borne out by recent events. China's neighbours in South-east Asia may be too politically divided to prevent China pursuing its nationalist agenda. To the extent that China has had a security dialogue with the Association of South-East Asian Nations (ASEAN) states, it has dealt with generalities. In the meantime China has continued to assert control over its claimed territory in the South China Sea and refuses to discuss shared sovereignty.[35] South-east Asians have improved economic relations with China, but increasingly worry about having to 'pay tribute' to a China that grows strong. Their interests would no doubt be better served by finding new ways to use their trading relations with China's coastal regions to nudge China into more neighbourly political relations.

Japan

Once Hong Kong is assimilated into China, Japan will emerge as China's largest trade partner. In 1991 it accounted for some 16% of Chinese trade, and the same percentage of China's total provincial trade. But just as there are special links between Taiwan, Hong Kong and southern China, so there is an evolving northern coastal NET. In 1990 Japan ranked first as the destination for exports from four Chinese provinces (Liaoning, Shandong, Qinghai and Xinjiang), and second for a further 20 provinces. Liaoning and Qinghai had high trade dependency ratios, while Shandong and Xinjiang were near the national average. Some 28% of total provincial exports to Japan were accounted for by exports from Liaoning – the obvious nexus of the northern coastal NET. Japanese relations were also particularly close in the Shanghai/Jiangsu region.

Comparing the trade figures for 1987 and 1990 suggests little change in the pattern of Japanese trade. In September 1992, 20 Japanese firms joined together to develop a special industrial park and half the foreign direct investment in Liaoning came from Japan. Some two-thirds of all foreign investment in Dalian came from Japan, in part because of the persistence of Japanese expertise on the region, as well as a large number of Chinese in Dalian who still spoke Japanese. The historical record of Japanese involvement can be a problem since many memories remain of harsh Japanese rule, but at a time of competition between China's cities and provinces for investment, past memories are often suppressed to ensure contemporary advantage.[36]

Despite the emergence of a northern coastal NET, there has been far less discussion of its importance compared to that of southern China. There are many reasons for this, one of them being the role of South Korea in the region (see below), but another is to be found in Japan's twentieth-century history. Having already occupied vast parts of China in the 1930s and 1940s and spent years trying to divide and manipulate it, modern Japanese are rightly careful about being accused of harbouring similar intentions now.

This delicacy about the past which hinders discussion about the present and future is, in fact, part of a broader and more serious problem in Sino-Japanese relations.[37] It is clear that each country sees the other as a problem in the post-Cold War world, and yet officials are reluctant to speak in public about the risks they perceive. Optimistic Japanese speak of their ability to control China by weaving it into webs of interdependence. Some Japanese even speak of their ability to manipulate China because Tokyo controls access to high technology and finance. But as Japan itself changes, so it expresses concern about a China unchecked by other powers. Recent projections about the size of the Chinese economy only fuel Japanese worries. They are concerned about the military dimensions of Sino-Japanese relations as China acquires in-flight refuelling or possibly even aircraft carriers.

They wonder why China wants to enter into long-term defence-production arrangements with Russia when there are no major threats to Chinese security. They puzzle over why China's defence budget is growing while nearly all other great powers are reducing theirs. Why does China criticise Japan's modest plans to take part in United Nations (UN) peacekeeping forces, while Beijing is reluctant to see Japan join the roster of permanent members of the UN Security Council? Could it be that China is trying to keep Japan from becoming a more normal power and trying to reassert the traditional role of Chinese preeminence? In 1993 Japan and China agreed to resume a high-level security dialogue, broken off in 1989, which may help ease some of the tensions in the relationship.[38] Other potential disputes include the damage done to the Japanese environment by pollution from China – a problem that is bound to grow as the Chinese economy expands.[39] Concrete confidence-building measures and a wider dialogue on multilateral issues are clearly necessary.

If Japan views China as seeking a more hegemonic role, then Tokyo may well rethink its economic and technological assistance to it. Might Japan seek closer Group of Seven (G-7) cooperation over policy towards China? Will Japan continue to put its trust in American protection and in its own ability to manage China through economic interdependence? To some extent the question is also whether Japan is prepared to work with other East Asians in dealing with a rising China. As Japanese economic interdependence is focused on the northern coastal NET, Japan has the potential either to work with other major players in other NETs, or to go it alone. By working together, but in separate NETs, China's neighbours, including Japan, will have the opportunity to make different parts of China compete for the favours of the outside world. Japan has leverage, but there are reasons why it will find it difficult to articulate an explicit strategy that seeks to make use of the regional differences in China. Nevertheless, there are ways in which Japan can maintain a formal dialogue with Beijing, while developing new forms of influence in the regions in the hope of moderating Chinese behaviour.

Korea

Korea, sometimes described as 'the Palestine of East Asia' because of claims by rival empires, sits uneasily between Japan and China. As a divided country it was also a battleground in the Cold War. It was only in the 1980s that China began to explore potential economic relations with South Korea, and relegated North Korea to a containment zone because of its economic backwardness and its odd and uncooperative policies. As Sino-North Korean trade dropped sharply, Sino-South Korean trade increased rapidly. Yet China's trade with South Korea has only recently become direct and diplomatic relations between them were only established in 1992. There has been insufficient time for an economic NET to be established, although given the relatively small size of the South Korean economy this may not really be formed until after the two Koreas are reunified.

For the time being, Sino-South Korean relations are best seen as part of the larger northern coastal NET led by Japan. China describes this as the Bohai Rim and claims it has the potential to rival the growth zones in the south or around Shanghai. China's trade with South Korea stood at some $5bn in 1992. There is a strong regional focus to that trade, most notably with the provinces of Shandong, Liaoning and Jilin. The Korean Autonomous Prefecture of Yanbian has a large concentration of Korean nationals (850,000) and in 1991 claimed to have sent one-third of its total export volume (or $4m) to South Korea. China's first ethnic-minority economic-development zone was created in the Yiyuan county of Shandong in order to attract Korean investment.[40] The much larger and more prosperous Liaoning province has been the largest provincial trade partner with South Korea. Trade has mostly been with smaller Korean companies who are most desperate for China's cheaper labour costs, although Beijing continues to hope that the larger Korean Chaebol will eventually become involved and make it easier for Beijing to manage the trade from afar.[41]

There are few prospects for South Korea, or even a unified Korea, evolving an especially powerful NET on its own. Neither is Korea likely to work well with Japan in a northern coastal NET because of the already wary state of their relations. As a result, China and its provinces have far more leverage and opportunity to play off one partner against the other than in any other NET. The Japanese and Koreans are likely to be competitors for Chinese favours and therefore all levels of the Chinese government may well find that they are able to drive tougher bargains on trade and technology transfer terms by encouraging the Japanese and Koreans to outbid each other. China also exerts important influence on North Korea, and as both South Korea and Japan grow more concerned about succession in Pyongyang and the risks of nuclear conflict, China's diplomatic leverage becomes more important. While there may eventually be prospects of a NET that includes what was once North Korea, China will retain important leverage over Japan and South Korea. As a result, South Koreans are finding that not all of China's neighbours can make use of regionalism in China. Similar conclusions are evident on China's most northern frontier with Russia.

Russia/Mongolia

There is perhaps no other bilateral relationship for China that is both so important and so ambivalent as that with Russia. As the Soviet Union, and in earlier days as Russia, China's northern neighbour has been both close comrade-in-arms and most evil of enemies. In the 1950s it was far and away China's major trade partner, but by the 1970s the Soviet Union might as well not have existed when considering patterns of Chinese trade. All those extremes were unnatural, but because they have existed so recently, there is little firm guidance on the normal state of Sino-Russian relations.

Current trade relations are distorted by the legacies of the past and the chaos in modern Russia. The total trade volume in 1991 was some $4bn, rising to $7.7bn in 1993. Total provincial export volume was $1.5bn in 1990. As might be expected for a country whose trade with East Asia was heavily focused on the north-east, Russia's trade with China could be narrowed down to very few provinces.[42] Although Russia ranked third for six Chinese provinces, it only ranked second for one (Xinjiang) and first for two others (Inner Mongolia and Heilongjiang). Trade as a percentage of GNP was low for Inner Mongolia (3.2%) and a bit higher for Heilongjiang (4.2%). Both had trade dependencies above the national average, but not exceptionally high.

From Russia's point of view, trade had grown more localised since the 1980s. This is primarily because of changes in the pattern of trade by Chinese provinces, as only the northern bordering provinces had an enduring need for trade with Russia because trade became based more on market forces than on state command. But even in 1990 Heilongjiang was the major provincial trade partner, followed by Shandong, Jilin, Jiangsu and only then Inner Mongolia. Whether this less than tightly knit trade along China's northern frontier constituted a NET is in part a matter of degree. Certainly there were distinctive trade orientations for northern provinces towards Russia, but they were not very strong when compared to the northern coastal and southern NETs. As Womack has suggested, many of these inland frontier connections are thin.

Perhaps these connections are just underdeveloped, at least in the case of Heilongjiang's connection with Russia. With 50,000 Chinese working and trading on the Russian side of the frontier and a good basis for economic complementarity, there are decent prospects for growth in trade. In 1992 a number of new towns and counties were given special status in order to enhance trade prospects. As in other parts of China, the decentralisation process often meant that economic decision-making was devolved well below the provincial level.[43] What problems there were seemed to stem primarily from the uncertainty and economic difficulties on the Russian side of the frontier. Nevertheless, border trade increased to $6bn in 1993, five times the 1991 figure, and new rail and air links were established. There was much talk (and a great deal of hype) about the prospects of multilateral cooperation in the Tumen River region that would bring Japanese capital to help exploit Chinese labour and Russian and North Korean resources. But given the serious concerns about the economic viability of the projects already discussed, let alone fundamental uncertainty about Korean politics and even the shape of Russia, it is not surprising that the discussions on the Tumen project never developed very far.[44]

But Russia has good reason to be wary of China as a unified great power. The relatively small Russian population in the Far East sitting on top of valuable natural resources feels highly vulnerable. It would feel even more so if Russia should fragment further and not have the protection of what is left of the Russian armed forces. If China grows fast it will require precisely those minerals and energy resources that are so close to it in the Russian Far East, and Russia knows it took much of this territory from a weak China in earlier centuries.

Perhaps for those reasons there is tension in Russia's view of China. On the one hand, in 1992 Russia sold 27 Su-27 aircraft and 144 aviation missiles and has since discussed a number of other possible ways for the defence industries of the two countries to collaborate. (Russian engineers are apparently working in various parts of the Chinese military industry.)[45] On the other hand, longer-term fears about Chinese intentions are fed by the infiltration of Chinese smugglers across the open frontier, and the piratical actions of Chinese officials and bandits in Pacific waters.[46] Decentralisation of policy on the Russian side, in the form of the break-up the Soviet Union, is also responsible for the failure to reach a border agreement.[47] But there are also longer-term worries in Russia about the wisdom of becoming too close militarily with China.

It has been argued in Russia that in the medium and longer term, China rather than Japan is Russia's main enemy in the region and that Russia and Japan thus need to work more closely together. Russia may be so weak in its Far Eastern territory that it may grow ever more wary of China. Major economic development in the Far East may require large-scale Chinese involvement, but to do so would make Russia highly dependent on China. At a minimum, while there are prospects for closer economic cooperation and the formation of a tighter NET in the region, Russia will find itself the weaker partner. Neither can Mongolia be of much help for it is even more dependent on, and vulnerable to, China.[48] The prospects are more for Chinese pressure on Russia than the other way around.

Central Asia

A geopolitician with anthropological training might see great potential for a NET in Central Asia that straddles Xinjiang and the newly independent states of the former Soviet Union, even as far as the frontiers of the Middle East.[49] With major ethnic populations on both sides of the frontiers, the basis for cooperation seems obvious. Yet such speculation is much too premature, given the basic uncertainty in the Central Asian states about their statehood and priorities. By contrast, the Chinese side of the frontier appears to be an area of relative tranquillity and prosperity.

There are millions of minority peoples and Muslims with affiliations across the frontier in the new Central Asian states. In all the important cases, the larger portion of the minority was on the former Soviet side of the frontier, except for the Uygurs (only 185,000 on the Kazakh side). Illegal immigration of up to 100 Chinese each day in 1993 to Kazakhstan has already been reported.[50] The Kazakhs across the border worry about being swamped and losing control of their economy, although they recognise that the level of Chinese technology may be better suited than that from the West. The Chinese model of economic and political reform also has its attractions for those in Central Asia who like the notion of 'enlightened authoritarianism'.[51] In 1992 total Chinese–Kazakh trade was $430m or 21% of Kazakhstan's total trade. By 1993 China had become Kazakhstan's major trade partner (after Russia), accounting for roughly 27% of imports and 20% of Kazakh exports. Discussions have been held about setting up a special economic zone, including the participation of Hong Kong companies.[52]

There is every expectation that China will remain a major trade partner for the Central Asian states. Beijing sees a possible NET as one led by itself and would hope to extend it further across the region to Pakistan, a long-standing ally of China. Both Urumqi and Beijing recognise that they are just starting out on this road of widening contacts in the region, but the tone of the initiative is distinctly confident. China's talk of a 'golden opportunity' may be optimistic, but it does reflect the feeling that it has the economic initiative in the region.[53]

As noted above, there are reasons for China to be wary about the openness implied in a Central Asian NET. Under certain circumstances, China could find its problems with its minorities growing, especially if economic growth in Xinjiang cannot be sustained. The fact that China changed its policy on Kashmir in 1993 to one that no longer supported the notion of self-determination for a mainly Muslim population, suggests serious Chinese concern with what its own Muslim population across the border might learn.[54] But under current conditions the prospects of a NET in either the north or west look far more likely to play into Beijing's hands than to serve the interests of those hostile to Chinese unity. Only conditions of privation in China's regions, or drastic decay and disarray in the centre, would work against China's interests.

The new Central Asian states bordering China all have deep, and probably growing, worries about Chinese intentions. President Nazarbayev of Kazakhstan is openly concerned about China's intentions in allowing large numbers of migrants to cross the frontier from Xinjiang. He also worries about China's nuclear capability and has noted that it has territorial claims against his country. In fact China has long-standing territorial claims to Tajikistan and Kyrgyzstan as well and officials can often be heard musing about China's long-term intentions.[55] Kyrgyz officials routinely blame China for natural disasters – for example, the earthquake in April 1992 was popularly believed to have been deliberately caused by a nuclear test in Lop Nor. In 1993 President Nazarbayev obtained China's agreement for a mechanism to monitor nuclear radiation from Lop Nor.[56] In short, the new Central Asian states seem more worried than the Chinese about the risks of closer relations in a Central Asian NET.

The brief surveys of these prospective northern and western NETs make clear that the implications of interdependence around China's rim can differ widely. In the north and west, the relative poverty and disarray of China's neighbours make the Chinese regions less subject to pull factors. China's south-western frontier with Myanmar and Vietnam is a difficult case because central government control is lacking on all sides. The most ominous challenge for Beijing is along coastal China, and primarily in the southern NET. The challenge is in fact that of neighbours who are rich and serve as poles of attraction. When coupled with rising aspirations in parts of China connected by these NETs, the challenge is powerful and growing. In short, China is both pushed and pulled in very different directions, but there is no doubt that the definition of the future shape of China is in flux.

III. CHINA CHANGES SHAPE

There are two central conclusions to this paper. First, important forces for change in China (particularly economic) and the outside world have led to a major decentralisation of certain types of power and to uncertainty about how China is and will be governed. Second, these new forces have led to significant alterations in the way the Chinese in China deal with the outside world. This concluding chapter assesses these two trends and identifies useful ways in which the outside world may better cope with the new China.

Forces for change

The signs that China is changing shape are increasingly clear. A closer look at its national identity reveals fissures and pressures that have long been masked by an official determination to uphold the myth of national unity. Yet rapid and radical economic reforms are transforming the structure of the Chinese economy and have even begun to affect its political system. These reforms are taking place at a time of the greatest uncertainty about the leadership of China since the communists came to power in 1949. As the central leadership loses some of its influence through the decentralisation of economic and some political power, it is harder for it to keep China's minorities in place. Chinese unity is also challenged by forces outside the country. Perhaps the most surprising pull on the national fabric comes from the overseas Chinese who are keen for parts of China to compete in the global market economy. The overseas Chinese are part of the broader process of international interdependence. By pulling parts of coastal China into different relationships, these forces are helping to form NETs.

Evidence shows that the central government in Beijing first surrendered power willingly, but in recent years has discovered how difficult it is to recover that power when it wishes to do so. Some key decisions on how to run the economy can no longer be enforced by Beijing and to the extent that managing economic success is an important part of the regime's legitimacy, and hence a key part of its political power, the decentralisation of economic power is also a decentralisation of political power. Indeed, it would be strange for a Communist Party leadership to argue that economics and politics could be anything but closely linked.

Yet evidence has also made clear that power has not simply been transferred to another player, for example a provincial leadership. Power has been devolved to a range of actors, including township and village enterprises, individuals and even overseas Chinese and other outsiders. Thus there is no simple struggle for control between centre and province.

Provincial leaders are aware of the relative increase in their powers, although their jousting with the centre and other levels of government is not generally manifest in formal statements. But interprovincial protectionism, trade wars and the refusal to accept central decisions on the economy, all suggest that real disputes exist and that real power has increased at the provincial level. Provincial trade with the outside world has also grown rapidly, while interprovincial trade has decreased in real terms. This is because the outside world is often a more reliable (not to mention more profitable) partner. As the World Bank suggests, China's provinces are becoming more independent actors.

One important reason why power has not flowed back to Beijing is the uncertainty surrounding the succession to Deng, and the state of factional politics. A central feature of the analysis here has been the extent to which the mixture of sweeping reforms and impending succession struggles has made officials at all levels wary of how they express their loyalties. This has resulted in signs of social decay, as well as a reluctance to restore powers to a central government that may not last very long. It makes little sense for the leaders of a reforming province along China's coast to make major sacrifices for the centre when it is not yet known who will be wielding power or controlling money in Beijing over the years to come.

Reshaping foreign relations
In an age of increasingly close links between domestic and foreign policy, major changes in China's domestic affairs have a significant impact on foreign relations. Thus China's relations with the outside world have changed, but in different ways for different parts of the country. This process has four levels.

First, Beijing has quite deliberately decentralised decisions on some issues. The vast increase in legitimate cross-border trade has led to the creation of different types of NETs. Whether in Central Asia, along the northern frontier or along the coast, cross-border trade has boomed. Even though much of this trade is outside central control, Beijing does not mind. Similarly, Beijing is generally pleased with its creation of special economic zones and has used their very diversity to ensure that no one region grows too strong. In short, not all decentralisation has had unwanted consequences for Beijing.

Second, and at the core of this study, are the unwanted consequences of decentralisation. Because such a range of China's economic interactions with the outside world has developed outside Beijing's control, the centre has found that it has worryingly little control over some key elements of its foreign economic policy. In some aspects of its foreign relations power has simply been decentralised and no one, except assorted individuals acting independently, has taken up that power. These include the sharp increase in problems with piracy, unsanctioned migration (even to the USA), the drug trade and gun running. Many of these problems result from Beijing's decision not to micro-manage border controls in order to encourage greater foreign trade. Any market economy often has such unsavoury features, but in the current Chinese case the results create a whole series of problems for central and regional government. Uncontrolled migration affects relations with neighbours, as well as countries as far away as Australia or the United States. Piracy has worried neighbours and upset the international community anxious to maintain open sea lanes. The gun and drug trades also affect social order right across China, as well as provoking complaints from neighbours from Central Asia to Hong Kong.

Unwanted consequences of decentralisation are also evident in evolving trade and investment relations, especially along the coast. China now finds that the United States has enormous leverage on it because investors from Hong Kong and Taiwan have ensured that the Chinese trade surplus with the United States remains huge. What is more, the trade practices of these enterprises along the coast are often beyond the control of central government. Beijing may sign international agreements on textile exports, protecting intellectual property or halting trade subsidies, but the central authorities are unable to control the violations of such accords. China may wish to join GATT and be ready to accept its rules on trade transparency, but provincial and township authorities are unwilling to be equally transparent in their dealings with Beijing, let alone the outside world. In short, China's ability to enforce accords on its own territory is affected by the decentralisation of economic power, as is its international reputation.

There are also strong signs that greater power for the regions and greater involvement of key NETs, including Hong Kong or Taiwan, have begun to affect Chinese policy towards parts of the outside world. China's ability to browbeat Hong Kong into accepting its political or constitutional terms is circumscribed in part by the new power Hong Kong exerts over the economy of southern China. More disconcerting for Beijing is that, as the regions grow stronger, Taiwan becomes less likely to unite with a non-unified mainland. On the contrary, Taiwan is more likely to exert a 'pull' of its own on coastal China. As Taiwan emerges as a more independent actor, it encourages greater independence of mind in those areas of China with which it deals.

Third, conditions are being created that may cause the centre to lose further control if the process of decentralisation continues. For example, as Japanese trade becomes increasingly focused on neighbouring parts of coastal China, and as Japan grows increasingly concerned about Chinese military power, there may be an increase in the as yet small number of people tempted to use Japan's economic influence to encourage parts of coastal China to moderate Beijing's political ambitions. Similar sentiments are beginning to be heard in South-east Asia about the virtues of interdependence in tying China down.

In Central Asia or Tibet, the risks of decentralisation are of a very different kind. Here, local elite groups, while beholden to Beijing, are aware of the serious potential for unrest on the part of local people. Greater economic decentralisation provides greater prosperity, but also rising expectations and rising resentment of foreign rule. As coastal China develops more political and economic power, the national bonds are loosened still further. This is not to say that regional separatists in Central Asia will lead the movement for change, but it does suggest that Chinese leaders have good reason to be worried about what they acknowledge to be increasingly powerful 'separatist tendencies'.

Fourth, it should be acknowledged that, for many aspects of Chinese foreign policy, the centre continues to hold great power. If the outside world wants to negotiate arms control or obtain a Chinese vote on the UN Security Council, they will have to talk to Beijing. So far there is no sign that regionalism has affected these aspects of foreign policy.

The centre is also apparently in control of such issues as human-rights policy and defence spending. Yet even on these issues there may soon be a greater independent role for the provinces. If foreign governments increasingly slap embargoes on exports from prisons, for example, the vested interests concerned are both local and national. The structure of defence spending may be affected the more the economy is decentralised and large defence manufacturers seek to convert to civil production for export. It has already been suggested that the foreign sales of the defence industry are often the result of local initiative or the actions of well-connected individuals.

What should be done?
How can the outside world handle this Muddle Kingdom? The new reality of China requires the outside world to adopt a more complex policy if it wishes to be effective. The forces at work are primarily

within China, but outsiders can be effective at the margins of this process of change. Any analysis of what the outside world should do must satisfy those who would ask 'to what end?' As has been posited, the strategic goals of outsiders will vary depending on their national interest and the part of China with which they are dealing. Trade relations are especially differentiated. But most outsiders will agree on the desirability of encouraging a China that is peacefully interdependent with the world beyond its borders. A goal of more complex interdependence will be harder to manage than if China had remained more centrally run. If China manages to hold together, even if only as a looser system, the outside world will find it easier to fashion more differentiated policies to suit specific interests. As China itself changes, the world has to face a new reality, and by adapting policy, this new reality can be made to suit basic Western goals towards China. To do nothing in the face of these major changes in China would be to retain an outdated China policy, to miss new opportunities and to fail to deal with new problems that emerge as decentralisation changes China's domestic and foreign policy.

Although the nature of decentralisation means that different countries will have more specialised trade relations with China, this does not mean that there will be more disputes among outsiders on how to handle China. Disputes about whether to pursue human rights or arms control as the priority will continue to divide outside governments, not to mention causing division within and between individual ministries. Similarly, debates about public or private diplomacy will continue. Regionalism in China adds yet another layer to these debates. For example, while some in the United States might seek to exert strong public pressure on coastal provinces to encourage Beijing to adopt a more accommodating attitude towards Hong Kong or territorial disputes, Japan and the ASEAN states might prefer to be more private and subtle in their diplomacy. The point is that all outsiders will increasingly adapt the way they deal with China to take into account the impact and opportunities of decentralisation.

It will be very difficult to develop and articulate a policy for dealing with a less centralised China that will not be interpreted in Beijing as an attempt to divide the country. There is no easy way around this problem, although China's own rhetoric about the virtues of decentralisation can be used to make the strategy of dealing in a less centralised fashion with a decentralising China more palatable. At least three clusters of policies can be identified, with many possible variations on, and connections between, them.

First, remarkably little is known about the localities, provinces and regions of China and far more needs to be known. How do the new institutions and interest groups operate? Who are the new individuals who benefit from decentralisation and who benefits most from imports or exports? At what point does the centre pass power down to the localities and when does it become harder to take that power back? What role do foreigners play in these struggles? This involves more study of local culture (including language), as well as local economic and political conditions. Far more needs to be known about local political and military elite groups and how they relate both to other regions and to the centre. Few of these questions are asked systematically and only a small number of Sinologists are working on the foreign-policy dimensions of decentralisation. Sinologists have curiously mirrored their country of study by also tending to accept relatively uncritically the myth of a unified national identity. It is no longer enough to go to Beijing and talk to officials in central government to understand events in a wider entity called China. Far more may be learned about real economic policy in all its facets by visiting Guangzhou or Shanghai. Nor is it any longer possible to visit any one part of China and come away with much more than a local snapshot.

Second, governments are already finding it necessary to develop far more local expertise. This involves the more expensive process of establishing and maintaining consulates or trade offices around China and in the parts of Asia connected to it by NETs. Governments are often reluctant to do this because of high staff costs at a time when funds and staff must be found for the new states that are emerging in Europe and Central Asia. China might even be reluctant to agree to the opening of more consulates or trade offices. An obvious answer, especially for like-minded states, would be to pool resources, especially outside the major coastal cities where the business opportunities are greatest. Similar arrangements are already made for new representation in Eastern Europe and Central Asia, and Australia and Canada agreed in September 1993 to establish shared facilities in many Asian and Latin American countries.

The purpose of such new consulates or trade offices would be both vastly to improve the range of information on local conditions and officials, and to support investment and trade in the region. It has long been inappropriate to assess China's economy in a centralised way and it similarly makes little sense to confine political and military analysis of China to staff in Beijing. For some purposes, a visit to Beijing is no more essential than it is for a Japanese investor in the United States to visit Washington when seeking to choose between a green-field site in

Tennessee or California. There is a great deal that localities can do to encourage foreign investment without angering Beijing, especially if it is kept below the current ceiling of $50m before Beijing's permission is required. Foreign lending institutions already often think in these regional terms.

These reforms in the way the outside world handles China will also require changes in foreign ministries where there will be a need for more staff and more complex decision-making procedures. Such a policy will not necessarily be opposed by Beijing for, as has already been seen, greater transparency on GATT issues or observation of intellectual property rules are supported by Beijing, even though they may be violated at the lower levels. By encouraging international business to think in terms of a more decentralised China, it will be easier to achieve the kinds of changes desired by the international community. So long as it is a goal of Western policy, a China that is more open to liberal political ideals or to international trade can be achieved both by dealing with Beijing, and by dealing with new centres of power in the regions. Thinking in such decentralised terms would only be a recognition of reality, and as a result provide better prospects for international trade and a more open China. Of course, governments should be wary about tampering with market forces, especially when overseas Chinese investment is far more sophisticated than most outside governments could possibly be. The need to think regionally is more a problem for Western investors who lack the local connections of the overseas Chinese.

Third, foreign governments can begin to treat China's provinces or regions as more independent levels of government, and to do so would merely be to recognise the new reality. This is not just a matter of information gathering, although that is essential. It is also a matter of evolving new policies that encourage China's provinces to feel more confident about their own position and ability to deal with the outside world. Broadcasting to China might be targeted more specifically at regional and local elite groups in order to provide less biased information about the course of decentralisation at home and the interests of foreigners abroad. From the point of view of the outside world, such policies would allow the point to be put across more directly, and provide more information about how decisions are taken at the increasingly important local level. Just as such information is needed about newly decolonised states or newly liberated ones in Eastern Europe or the former Soviet Union, so the outside world needs to know more about the thinking and operation of new actors in the international system, even if they happen still to be within China's frontiers.

Regional leaders in neighbouring countries, for example in Japan or South Korea, might establish regular channels of communication with provincial leaders in China. This should go beyond the usual banalities of twinning cities, and include funding of exchange programmes on technical and cultural matters. Regular channels might even be established to discuss such security issues as piracy or environmental matters such as pollution. By establishing more regular connections, greater openness would be developed. Aid given to regional broadcasters could be especially helpful in this regard. The basic desire should be to understand the new diversity and perhaps help shape it in ways that meet foreigners' needs. The West already expresses this desire in its policies towards Beijing, for example, on human rights or trade policy, so it is only sensible to extend this policy to the new centres of power at the local level. If outsiders wish to end exports by Chinese enterprises which violate intellectual property regulations, use prison labour or violate GATT regulations by benefiting from massive injections of capital from local government, their policies need to be tailored to reach China's local levels.

An expanded range of openness to local leaders might also include extending invitations to them to be guests of other governments, perhaps supported by 'know-how' fund projects for training, as Europeans currently do for Eastern Europeans. Assistance to China in the form of development aid or even educational grants and exchange programmes might be established at the provincial or even lower levels, rather than exclusively at the national level, thereby building more specific networks of influence. As China becomes more open, there are new opportunities for more varied contacts. In good times this enhancement of openness at local levels will be good for trading interests. In bad times, for example if centre–local relations should deteriorate sharply, the outside world will know more about the process and be better able to judge what policies might be more appropriate. These provincial officials should be specifically invited to join national delegations visiting other countries and take part in events sponsored by international institutions. Identification of the people involved should be done by foreign governments and not left to the nomenklatura system of the Beijing regime.

The most controversial aspect of a greater international status for Chinese provinces is the way in which provincial governments may need to be consulted on security issues. While it is true that most issues on the international-security agenda will still be dealt with on the national level – for example, arms control or UN peacekeeping – it is possible that efforts undertaken at the provincial level to reinforce messages delivered in Beijing may well be worth considering.

States that worry about China's possible use of force, whether against Taiwan or in the South China Sea, could encourage local leaders in southern China to realise that they may suffer a loss of investment and prosperity if they do not urge Beijing to limit its ambitions. Japan might send a similar message to coastal China if it should wish to use its influence to encourage China to avoid a military build-up. Provinces with large defence industries might be given special aid to convert to civilian industry. Provinces with factories producing exports using prison labour might be targeted for international pressure, just as complaints are lodged at the national level. In short, provinces can be singled out for special treatment both in the area of incentives and penalties.

Into the beyond
Given the complexity of the internal and external forces involved, it is impossible to be certain about the future shape of China. A return to rigidly centralised rule is highly unlikely, but should not be entirely ruled out. Nor should a break-up of China be entirely ruled out. There are certainly powerful forces that could explain such a development, especially at a time of major uncertainty about the succession to Deng Xiaoping. When examining what held states together (the USA in the 1860s) or allowed them to split (the USSR in the 1990s), the final outcome was rarely obvious from the start. But what does appear clear is that, even though external forces have helped pull at the fabric of China, they will not be a determining factor in any specific crisis that might emerge. The fate of China will be in the hands of the Chinese and will depend critically on how they manage their reforms. If things go badly for the centre, the outside world may fear the calamitous consequences of mass migration or worry about damage to the international economy, but some would also applaud the end of 'the China threat'.

The most likely outcome is a prolonged crisis of national identity, where changes short of complete collapse have an important impact on the lives of the Chinese and their neighbours. The preceding analysis has argued that China's crisis is in part the result of the failure of the old ideology and the consequent failure to evolve a new and coherent system for governing the country. It may be that the country is simply heading into a more chaotic era, or what optimists might prefer to call pragmatic government. But the evidence also suggests that this is not just a crisis of the regime; it has important elements of a crisis of national identity.

The notion that China faces a crisis of national identity has led some dissidents to discuss the role that federalism might play in a new China.[1] As noted above, Chinese debates about federalism some 70 years ago were stifled by the outbreak of warlordism. Current discussions of federalism stress the advantages that might be obtained from a looser form of government that allows for the incorporation of the more liberal ideas of government found in Taiwan and Hong Kong. They are in part an antidote to the discussions of 'new authoritarianism' that were supported by some of Zhao Ziyang's associates before his purge in 1989. The discussions represent the restoration to Chinese political thought of the debate on how to reconcile the Great and Little Traditions.[2]

Yet it is unlikely that China will adopt a formally federal structure. A crucial component to effective federalism is a firm legal tradition and Confucian political culture lacks anything of the sort. Indeed, one of the key features that distinguishes East Asian from transatlantic political cultures is the relative absence in East Asia of legal forms for settling disputes and managing social relations. The implications of this are evident in everything from trade disputes to debates over human rights. Interestingly, there are virtually no countries in East Asia (apart from Malaysia) with a federal form of government.

There can, however, be informal variants of federalism. China might best be seen as evolving a distinctive type of informal federalism where power is managed in different ways at different levels, and even varies in form at the same level. It seems unlikely that a mechanism for government could be introduced, whether formal or informal, which could micro-manage or micro-administer such diversity. Whether one adopts the Euro-speak of 'subsidiarity' and 'variable geometry', or the political science concept of 'polycentrism', the reality in China is tending increasingly towards devolved power. Effective authority can now be found at very different levels, both within and outside China, depending on the specific issues at stake. This is already evident in much of China's foreign economic relations. The role of external power and authority is especially novel in Chinese history, for China has never been as interdependent with the outside world as it is today.

The motive for developing a more differentiated policy towards China is at least two-fold. First, it is clear that China is already decentralising key aspects of its policies, and it is simply prudent to be better prepared for this process and better able to manage change that is already taking place under the twin pressures of domestic and international forces. Even if the outside world undertook none of the steps outlined above, China would continue to decentralise power and change would be forced upon the outside world.

A second motive is simply that if China is left to manage its own regionalism it might only be able to contain fissiparous tendencies by strengthening its nationalist and irredentist policies. If China is left to grow economically strong and more ruthlessly nationalist at the same time, it is likely to be far more difficult for the outside world to deal with. The advantages of undertaking a more engaged attitude towards Chinese regionalism will be perceived in different ways by Beijing. On the one hand, the Chinese would be right in supposing that many foreign governments would welcome a more decentralised China because it would weaken Beijing's ability to pursue a nationalist agenda, for example as regards territorial disputes.

On the other hand, Beijing can also see ways in which the outside world can play a positive role in dealing with regionalism. If foreigners positively engage with the process of decentralisation, they might make a formal break-up less likely. A strategy of engagement with China's regions is intended to gain more information about the process and minimise the risks of chaos. On many issues, the outside world has an interest in a more decentralised China. But it also has an interest, at least on some issues (e.g., GATT or arms sales) in an effective government in Beijing. If the outside world seriously believes that it can best accommodate China's rising power by weaving it into webs of interdependence, then the strongest webs will be built on regional and local lines. The outside world has no interest in the formal break-up of China. But there is much that stops short of a formal break-up which offers the outside world the opportunity of creating a more realistic and constructive dialogue with China. It may be that the only way to ensure that China does not become more dangerous as it grows richer and stronger is to ensure that in practice, if not in law, there is more than one China to deal with.

Notes

Introduction

[1] In official Chinese parlance it is legitimate to discuss 'decentralisation', but only in September 1993 were there signs of more open discussions of the foreign-policy implications of the process. See Li Danren in *Remin Ribao*, British Broadcasting Corporation, *Summary of World Broadcasts/Far East* (henceforth *FE*), 1612/B2/5-6, 10 February 1993, and the report of the Chinese Academy of Social Sciences, *International Herald Tribune* (henceforth *IHT*), 21 September 1993.

Chapter I

[1] Lucian Pye, 'China: Erratic State, Frustrated Society', *Foreign Affairs*, no. 4, 1990, p. 58. See also Benjamin Schwartz, 'Culture, Modernity and Nationalism – Further Reflections', *Daedalus*, Summer 1993.

[2] Lowell Dittmer and Samuel Kim, 'In Search of a Theory of National Identity', in Dittmer and Kim (eds), *China's Quest for National Identity* (Ithaca, NY: Cornell University Press, 1993).

[3] In the Arab world, or even in the Americas, a common script has not prevented the emergence of multiple states. See Benedict Anderson, *Imagined Communities* (London: Verso, 1991).

[4] Mark Elvin, *The Pattern of the Chinese Past* (Stanford, CA: Stanford University Press, 1973), John Fairbank, 'The Reunification of China', *The Cambridge History of China*, vol. 14 (Cambridge: Cambridge University Press, 1987), Ping-Ti Ho, 'The Chinese Civilization', *Journal of Asian Studies*, no. 35, 1976, William Skinner, 'The Structure of Chinese History', *ibid.*, no. 44, 1985, and Myron Cohen, 'Being Chinese', *Daedalus*, Spring 1991.

[5] Anderson, *Imagined Communities*, p. 50.

[6] Cohen, 'Being Chinese', especially pp. 121–26.

[7] Joseph Witney, *China: Area, Administration and Nation Building*, University of Chicago, Department of Geography, Research Paper no. 123, 1970.

[8] Wolfram Eberhard, 'Chinese Regional Stereotypes', *Asian Survey*, no. 12, 1965.

[9] Helen Siu, 'Cultural Identity and the Politics of Difference in South China', *Daedalus*, Spring 1993, and Lynn White and Li Chang, 'China's Coast Identities', in Dittmer and Kim (eds), *China's Quest*.

[10] See the pioneering work by Witney, *Area, Administration*.

[11] Wang Fuzhi quoted in Prasenjit Duara, 'De-Constructing the Chinese Nation', *The Australian Journal of Chinese Affairs*, no. 30, 1993, p. 7.

[12] Benjamin Schwartz, 'The Primacy of the Political Order in East Asian Societies', in Stuart Schram (ed.), *Foundations and Limits of State Power in China* (Hong Kong: Chinese University Press, 1987), and W. J. F. Jenner, *The Tyranny of History: The Roots of China's Crisis* (New York: Viking, 1992).

[13] Michael Ng-Quinn, 'National Identity in Premodern China', in Dittmer and Kim (eds), *China's Quest*.

[14] Joseph Levenson, *Modern China and its Confucian Past* (New York: Anchor Books, 1964), Tu Wei-ming, 'Cultural China', *Daedalus*, Spring 1991, Hugh Seton-Watson, *Nation and States* (London: Methuen, 1977), p. 148, and Anderson, *Imagined Communities*, especially chapter 10.

[15] Duara, 'De-Constructing', p. 12, and Michael Hunt, 'Chinese National Identity and the Strong State', in Dittmer and Kim (eds), *China's Quest*.

[16] Arthur Waldron, 'Warlordism Versus Federalism', *The China Quarterly*, no. 121, 1990, and Prasenjit Duara, 'Provincial Narratives of the Nation', in Harumi Befu (ed.), *Cultural National-*

ism in East Asia (Berkeley, CA: Institute of East Asian Studies, 1992).

[17] Samuel Kim and Lowell Dittmer, 'Whither China's Quest for National Identity?', in Dittmer and Kim (eds), *China's Quest*.

[18] James Townsend, 'Chinese Nationalism', *The Australian Journal of Chinese Affairs*, no. 27, 1992; Duara, 'De-Constructing'.

[19] Edward McCord, *The Power of the Gun* (Berkeley, CA: University of California Press, 1993), and Brantly Womack, 'Warlordism and Military Regionalism in China', *Pacific Review*, no. 1, 1994.

[20] Stuart Schram, 'Decentralization in a Unitary State', in Schram (ed.), *State Power*.

[21] Gerald Segal, *Defending China* (Oxford: Oxford University Press, 1985).

[22] Merle Goldman *et al.*, 'China's Intellectuals in the Deng Era', in Dittmer and Kim (eds), *China's Quest*.

[23] On *River Elegy,* see Su Xiaokang and Wang Luxiang, *Deathsong of the River* (Ithaca, NY: Cornell East Asia Series, 1991). The quote is from p. 116 and paraphrases Toynbee.

[24] Wang Gungwu, 'The Study of Chinese Identities in Southeast Asia', in Jennifer W. Cushman and Wang Gungwu (eds), *Changing Identities in Southeast Asian Chinese since World War II* (Hong Kong: Hong Kong University Press, 1988).

[25] Edward Friedman, 'A Failed Chinese Modernity', *Daedalus*, Spring 1993, and *New National Identities in Post-Leninist Transformations* (Hong Kong: Chinese University of Hong Kong, 1992).

[26] Cohen, 'Being Chinese', p. 133.

[27] This subject is a matter of some statistical quibbling. Reports of the trend were first given prominence in *The Economist*, 'A Survey of China', 28 November 1992, based on IMF and World Bank data, and a paper by Australian economists later published as Ross Garnaut and Guonan Ma, 'How Rich is China?', *The Australian Journal of Chinese Affairs*, no. 30, 1993. The Chinese Academy of Social Sciences, in conjunction with two American universities, agreed that China would lead economically in 2020. See *Xinhua*, in *FE*/W0278/A/1, 3 April 1993. See also *The Economist*, 15 May 1993 for updated data.

[28] David Goodman, 'The Political Economy of Regionalism in China', a paper prepared for the Australia–China Conference on Regionalism, July 1993.

[29] Classic discussion of these issues can be found in Franz Schurmann, *Ideology and Organization in Communist China* (Berkeley, CA: University of California Press, 1966), and Harry Harding, *Organizing China* (Stanford, CA: Stanford University Press, 1981). See also Jonathan Unger, 'The Struggle to Dictate China's Administration', *The Australian Journal of Chinese Affairs*, no. 18, 1987.

[30] Dorothy Solinger, *Regional Government and Political Integration in Southwest China, 1949–1954* (Berkeley, CA: University of California Press, 1977), p. 29, and Schram, 'Decentralization', pp. 100–1.

[31] This sections depends on Shaun Breslin, 'Changing Centre–Province Relations in the PRC in the 1980s', unpublished PhD thesis, Newcastle University, October 1993, and Gordon White, *Riding the Tiger* (London: Macmillan, 1993).

[32] David Goodman (ed.), *China's Regional Development* (London: Routledge for the RIIA, 1989).

[33] Maria Hsia Chang, 'China's Future: Regionalism, Federation, or Disintegration', *Studies in Comparative Communism*, no. 3, 1992, p. 215.

[34] *Far Eastern Economic Review*, 4 April 1991, p. 21.

[35] *Zhongguo Tongxun* (Hong Kong), 30 November 1992, Foreign Broadcast

Information Service (hereafter FBIS), CHI-92-241, 15 December 1992, pp. 41–42.

[36] Athar Hussein and Nicholas Stern, 'Economic Reforms and Public Finance in China', London School of Economics, China Programme, Paper no. 23, June 1992. See also *Wen Wei Po*, in *FE*/1843/G/5-6, 8 November 1993.

[37] See the Finance Minister's outlines of new tax reforms in *Xinhua*, *FE*/1850/G/ 5-6, 17 November 1993, and analysis in *The Economist*, 20 November 1993.

[38] *Ta Kung Pao* (Hong Kong), *FE*/ 1739/B2/1-2, 8 July 1993, *Xinhua*, *FE*/ 1822/G/1-2, 24 September 1993, *Liaowang*, no. 43, 25 October 1993, *FE*/1836/G/3-4, *The Economist*, 6 November 1993, and *IHT*, 30 October 1993.

[39] For an indication of the struggle and ways in which the regions were defying Beijing, see *Ming Pao* (Hong Kong), 24 December 1993, *FE*/1884/G/5-6.

[40] *South China Morning Post*, 23 June 1993, and *The Economist*, 26 June 1993.

[41] *IHT*, 9 July 1993.

[42] Zhu Rongji in *Xinhua*, 9 July 1993, *FE*/1741/B2/1-2, and *Xinhua*, 30 August 1993, *FE*/1782/G/1-3. See also *Financial Times*, 25 August 1993.

[43] *The Economist*, 26 June 1993.

[44] Chang, 'China's Future', p. 217.

[45] Junhua Wu, 'Economic Growth and Regional Development Strategy in China', *Japan Research Quarterly*, no. 3, 1993.

[46] *Xinhua*, 2 January 1994, *FE*/1886/G/ 7.

[47] *Far Eastern Economic Review*, 10 June 1993, pp. 54–59, and *IHT*, 7 April 1993.

[48] Gerald Segal, 'A Changing China and Asian/Pacific Security', paper prepared for the IISS–CAPS Conference, Hong Kong, June 1993.

[49] *Window* (Hong Kong), 25 June 1993, pp. 48–49.

[50] This material comes from work in

progress by the World Bank on China's internal market. It notes that in the 1985–92 period, overseas exports and imports grew at 17% and 10% respectively. Domestic interprovincial trade also rose in absolute terms, but its rate of growth at 4.8% per year was low relative to foreign trade and also lower than the 9% annual growth rate of total retail sales.

[51] *Ching Pao* (Hong Kong), 5 June 1993, *FE*/1715/B2/7.

[52] *Hsiang Kang Shang Pao* (Hong Kong), 5 October 1993, *FE*/1822/G/2.

[53] Details of these events are drawn from work currently underway by the World Bank. See also *Daily Telegraph*, 8 January 1991, and Chang, 'China's Future'.

[54] *Remin Ribao*, 24 October 1990, FBIS-CHI-90-213, 2 November 1990, pp. 26–28.

[55] The central government's effort began in 1986 and by October 1991 the total amount of capital involved was $375m. See *China Daily*, 17 October 1991, p. 1, and *Xinhua*, 14 May 1991, FBIS-CHI-91-097, 20 May 1991, p. 64. On recent failures, see *Xinhua*, 6 December 1993, *FE*/0312/WG/11.

[56] *Xinhua*, 15 July 1991, FBIS-CHI-91-137, 17 July 1991, p. 64.

[57] Xinjiang Television, 21 August 1991, FBIS-CHI-91-164, 23 August 1991, p. 50.

[58] Reported in *Tangtai* (Hong Kong), no. 63, 9 February 1991, FBIS-CHI-91-031, 14 February 1991, pp. 22–24.

[59] *China News Analysis*, no. 1463, 1 July 1992, p. 3.

[60] *The Economist*, 19 June 1993.

[61] David Goodman, 'The PLA and Regionalism in Guangdong', *Pacific Review*, no. 1, 1994.

[62] Wu, 'Economic Growth', p. 44.

[63] Goodman, 'The PLA and Regionalism in Guangdong'.

[64] This section relies on Peter Tsan-yin Cheung, 'The Evolving Relations Between the Center and Guangdong in

the Reform Era', unpublished paper, May 1993.

[65] David Goodman, 'Political Perspectives', in Goodman (ed.), *China's Regional Development*, p. 31.

[66] *South China Morning Post Weekly*, 28 August 1993, p. 4, and *Far Eastern Economic Review*, 2 September 1993, pp. 42–44.

[67] These issues are discussed in a special issue of *Pacific Review* on the new rich, no. 4, 1992, and in a paper on Guangdong by David Goodman prepared for the conference, 'China Deconstructs', Washington DC, October 1993.

[68] *China News Analysis*, no. 1463, 1 July 1992, p. 5.

[69] Interviews in Shanghai in June/July 1993.

[70] See, for example, *Shanghai Wen Hui Bao*, 15 January 1993, in FBIS-CHI-93-021, 3 February 1993, pp. 65–67.

[71] 'Shanghai Replays Role as an Oriental Metropolis', *Beijing Review*, 2–9 May 1993; but most of this section is based on local interviews in June/July 1993.

[72] See Michael Yahuda, 'The PLA and Regionalism in Manchuria', paper prepared for the IISS–CAPS conference, Hong Kong, June 1993.

[73] Womack, 'Warlordism', but especially Waldron, 'Warlordism Versus Federalism'.

[74] Ellis Joffe, 'Regionalism in China', *Pacific Review*, no. 1, 1994.

[75] On these issues in Deng's case, see David Goodman, *Deng Xiaoping* (London: Cardinal, 1990).

[76] The first such reference was in *China Youth News*. See Jonathan Mirsky, *The Times*, 7 January 1994.

[77] *Cheng Ming* (Hong Kong), no. 192, 1 October 1993, in *FE*/1819/G/2.

[78] *Xinhua*, 21 July 1993, in *FE*/1748/B2/1.

[79] *Ching Pao* (Hong Kong), no. 4, 5 April 1993, in FBIS-CHI-93-063, 5 April 1993, pp. 21–22.

[80] *Remin Ribao*, 10 February 1993, in FBIS-CHI-93-027, 11 February 1993, pp. 16–17.

[81] *The Standard* (Hong Kong), 8 May 1993, p. 1.

[82] Ellis Joffe, *The Chinese Army After Mao* (London: Weidenfeld and Nicolson, 1988).

[83] Michael Swaine, *The Military and Political Succession in China* (Santa Monica, CA: RAND, 1992).

[84] Ellis Joffe, 'Chinese Nationalism Guarantees Unity', *IHT*, 21 July 1993.

[85] This section relies on papers by Harlan Jencks and Peter Yu presented at the IISS–CAPS conference, Hong Kong, June 1993.

[86] See Swaine, *Political Succession*, for details.

[87] These arguments are developed in far greater detail in nearly all the papers presented at the IISS–CAPS conference, Hong Kong, June 1993.

[88] *Hsin Pao* (Hong Kong), 8 October 1993, in *FE*/1832/G/8-9, and Jiang Zemin as quoted in *Jiefangjun Bao*, 2 October 1993, in *FE*/1819/G/3-4.

[89] As in *Remin Ribao*, 26 July 1993.

[90] *Kuang Chiao Ching* (Hong Kong), no. 248, 16 May 1993, in *FE*/1710/B2/4-5.

[91] *Jiefangjun Bao*, 20 August 1992, in FBIS-CHI-92-177, 11 September 1992, pp. 46–47; *Xinhua*, 12 February 1993, in FBIS-CHI-93-028, 12 February 1993, p. 17; and *Xinhua*, 4 February, in FBIS-CHI-93-023, 5 February 1993, p. 12.

[92] *Xinhua*, 9 April 1993, in FBIS-CHI-93-074, 20 April 1993, p. 22, *Xinhua*, 13 April 1993, in FBIS-CHI-93-070, 14 April 1993, pp. 22–23, and generally Tai Ming Cheung, 'Economic Reform and PLA Regionalism', paper prepared for the IISS–CAPS conference, Hong Kong, June 1993. See his later report in *Far Eastern Economic Review*, 14 October 1993, pp. 64–71.

[93] See, for example, *Jiefangjun Bao*, 14 April 1993, in FBIS-CHI-93-085, 5

May 1993, pp. 18–19.

[94] *Xinjiang Ribao*, 12 February 1993, in FBIS-CHI-93-041, 4 March 1993, p. 16, and *Zhongguo Tongxun She*, 16 May 1993, in FBIS-CHI-93-094, 18 May 1993, p. 33.

[95] *Zhongguo Xinwen She*, 12 May 1993, in FBIS-CHI-93-091, 13 May 1993, as well as various reports in no. 078, 26 April 1993, p. 56. On the extra-budget earnings, see *Ming Pao* (Hong Kong), 3 February 1993, in FBIS-CHI-93-021, 3 February 1993, p. 27, and *South China Morning Post*, 9 March 1993, p. 10.

[96] *Ming Pao* (Hong Kong), 13 February 1993, in FBIS-CHI-93-033, 22 February 1992, p. 32. See also *Xinhua*, 8 February 1992, in FBIS-CHI-92-027, 10 February 1992, p. 30.

[97] Optimism in the early 1990s is evident in *Jiefangjun Bao*, 21 December 1991, in FBIS-CHI-92-008, 13 January 1992, pp. 39–43, or *Jiefangjun Bao*, 30 March 1992, in FBIS-CHI-92-074, 16 April 1992, pp. 35–39. This view was evident in analysis by Ellis Joffe, 'The PLA and the Succession Question', and David Shambaugh, 'The PLA and Internal Order', both in Richard Yang (ed.), *China's Military: The PLA in 1992–93* (Boulder, CO: Westview, 1993).

[98] These issues have been debated at length in various contributions in Richard Yang (ed.), *PLA Yearbook* (Boulder, CO: Westview, 1992).

[99] *Cheng Ming* (Hong Kong), 1 June 1993, in *FE/1706/A1/2-5*.

[100] *Xinhua*, 21 July 1992, in FBIS-CHI-92-141, 22 July 1992, p. 38, which reports only 55 different nationalities. The number 56 has been used more commonly recently. See a speech by Li Peng quoted in *Xinhua*, 18 January 1992, in FBIS-CHI-92-013, 21 January 1992, p. 25.

[101] *Far Eastern Economic Review*, 25 August 1988, p. 30, and *Ethnic Statistics of China, 1949–1990* (Beijing: Chinese Statistical Publishing Co., 1991).

[102] *Xinhua*, 21 May 1991, in FBIS-CHI-91-100, 23 May 1991, p. 35.

[103] Quoted by *Cheng Ming* (Hong Kong), no. 171, 1 January 1992, in FBIS-CHI-92-001, 2 January 1992, p. 28.

[104] S. A. M. Adshead, *Central Asia in World History* (London: Macmillan, 1993), p. 222.

[105] For example, Li Peng, reported by *Xinhua*, 18 January 1992, and *Remin Ribao*, 19 January, in FBIS-CHI-92-103, 21 January 1992, pp. 25–28. See also *China Daily*, 16 April 1992, p. 4.

[106] *Xinjiang Ribao*, 11 December 1993, in *FE/1886/G/8-11*.

[107] *Xinjiang Ribao*, 19 October 1990, in FBIS-CHI-90-222, 16 November 1990, pp. 67–70; Jiang in *Xinhua*, 7 November 1993, in *FE/1841/G/1-3*; and Ismail Amat on Xinjiang's People's Broadcasting Station, 8 November 1993, in *FE/1843/G/7*.

[108] Xinjiang Television, 25 May 1991, in FBIS-CHI-91-103, 29 May 1991, pp. 76–77, and *Xinjiang Ribao*, 18 May 1991, in FBIS-CHI-91-111, 10 June 1991, pp. 53–54.

[109] *Qinhai Ribao*, 2 October 1993, in *FE/1818/G/4-6*, and on 8 October in *FE/1823/G/3-4*. See also *The Times*, 30 October 1993.

[110] *Xinhua*, 23 May 1991, in FBIS-CHI-91-100, 23 May 1991, pp. 33–34, and Tibet Television (in Mandarin), 12 November 1992, in FBIS-CHI-92-223, 18 November 1992, pp. 28–29.

[111] Agence France Presse (AFP) in Hong Kong quoting the Tibet Party Secretary, 8 January 1993, in FBIS-CHI-93-005, 8 January 1993, p. 43, and the Governor of Tibet also quoted by AFP on 1 February 1993, in FBIS-CHI-93-019, 1 February 1993, pp. 56–57. Also TV Lhasa, 9 September 1993 in *FE/1800/G/2-4*.

[112] PTI News Agency, 3 October 1993, in *FE/1810/G/1*, and Tibet Broadcasting, Lhasa, 15 September, in *FE/1819/*

G/5-6.
[113] *Neimenggu Ribao*, 2 October 1993, in *FE*/1842/G/10-11. A sense of the more complacent tone can be seen in *Qiushi* (Beijing), no. 9, 1 May 1991, in FBIS-CHI-91-112, 11 June 1991, pp. 2021.
[114] *The Economist*, 18 July 1992.
[115] *Ibid*.
[116] Wang Gungwu, 'Among Non-Chinese', and David Yen-ho Wu, 'The Construction of Chinese and Non-Chinese Identities', *Daedalus*, Spring 1991.
[117] *The Economist*, 17 July 1993, and *Financial Times*, 15 December 1992.
[118] 'The Status of Overseas Chinese Studies', a paper prepared for the Luodi-Shenggen conference, November 1992.

Chapter II
[1] The NET is a useful concept because it stresses the extent to which contacts can develop despite existing internal and external frontiers. The strength of NETs can be 'measured' by the intensity of trade and financial flows, as well as by the movement of people or even ideas.
[2] There are huge problems with the data. Data on Chinese trade is skewed because of the problems of counting indirect trade with South Korea and Taiwan which used to pass mainly through Hong Kong. Smuggling has also increased in recent years along various frontiers. In short, the data should be taken as indicating trends rather than providing precise calculations. See Nicholas Lardy, *Foreign Trade and Economic Reform in China* (Cambridge: Cambridge University Press, 1992).
[3] Calculations in Brantly Womack and Guangzhi Zhao, 'The Many Worlds of China's Provinces: Foreign Trade and Diversification', paper prepared for the conference 'China Deconstructs', Washington DC, October 1993.
[4] These calculations are based on various years of the *Almanac of Chinese Foreign Economy and Trade*, cited in Stefan Landsberger, *China's Provincial Foreign Trade* (London: RIIA, 1989), and Womack and Zhao, 'The Many Worlds'.
[5] *China Daily*, 22 May 1993, p. 1.
[6] David Zweig, 'Internationalizing China's Countryside', *The China Quarterly*, no. 128, 1991, p. 718.
[7] Junhua Wu, 'Economic Growth and Regional Development Strategy in China', *Japan Research Quarterly*, no. 3, 1993.
[8] Womack and Zhao, 'The Many Worlds'.
[9] Zweig, 'Internationalizing China's Countryside', p. 718.
[10] Womack and Zhao, 'The Many Worlds'.
[11] David Zweig, 'Reaping Rural Rewards', *The China Business Review*, November–December 1992, pp. 12–17.
[12] Unless otherwise noted, this section relies heavily on Gerald Segal, *The Fate of Hong Kong* (London: Simon and Schuster, 1993).
[13] *Financial Times*, 19 December 1993.
[14] *Ming Pao* (Hong Kong), 30 June 1992, in FBIS-CHI-92-126, 30 June 1992, p. 17; *Zhongguo Tongxun* (Hong Kong), 13 May 1993, in FBIS-CHI-93-097, 21 May 1993, pp. 14–15; and *IHT*, 9 April 1993.
[15] *Wen Wei Po* (Hong Kong), 12 September 1993, in *FE*/1802/G/9-10.
[16] See, for example, the case of Liaoning, *Xinhua*, 19 October 1992, in FBIS-CHI-92-204, 21 October 1992, p. 49. See also *Zhongguo Tongxun She*, 13 May 1993, in *FE*/1702/B2/3.
[17] *Zhongguo Xinwen She*, 21 July 1993, in FE/1748/B2/4, and *The Economist*, 24 July 1993.
[18] David Goodman, *Southern China in Transition* (Canberra: AGPO, 1992).
[19] Goodman, 'The PLA and Regionalism', and *Financial Times*, 7 June 1993.

[20] *Xinhua*, 10 July 1993, in *FE/1739/ A2/1-2*, and *Far Eastern Economic Review*, 14 October 1993, p. 74.

[21] Ting Wai, 'The Regional and International Implications of the South China Economic Zone', *Issues and Studies*, December 1992.

[22] *IHT*, 27 April 1993, and *South China Morning Post Weekly*, 1 August 1993, p. 5.

[23] *Financial Times*, 27 April 1993. *Far Eastern Economic Review*, 20 May 1993, p. 66, puts the figure for total trade in 1992 at $14bn. For early 1993 data, see China News Agency, Taiwan, 24 May 1993, in FBIS-CHI-93-099, 25 May 1993, p. 55.

[24] *Far Eastern Economic Review*, 1 July 1993, pp. 21–22.

[25] *Asian Wall Street Journal*, 6 December 1993.

[26] *Xinhua*, 24 May 1993, in FBIS-CHI-93-099, 25 May 1993, p. 52.

[27] *Financial Times*, 14 May 1993.

[28] *Xinhua*, 11 July 1993, in *FE/1739/ A2/3-4*. Of course Lee pledged to consult with Beijing before making the decision. See reports of his Suzhou trip in *Xinhua*, 12 May 1993, in FBIS-CHI-93-099, 25 May 1993, p. 9.

[29] John Garver, 'China's Push Through the South China Sea', *The China Quarterly*, December 1992.

[30] Details on the Hong Kong debate are subject to the usual caveats about reading Chinese tea leaves. On the resort to nationalism among hardliners see, for example, *Chiushih Nientai* (Hong Kong), no. 5, 1 May 1993, in *FE/1681/B2/4-5*. See also Hong Kong's *Cheng Ming*, 1 January 1993, in *FE/ 1577/A2/3-7*, in the midst of the recent Sino-British row over Hong Kong.

[31] Michael Williams, *Vietnam* (London: Pinter for the RIIA, 1992). For more recent evidence of humiliation, see the violation of Vietnamese territorial waters by Chinese-sponsored oil drillers just before Chi Haotian visited Hanoi, *Far Eastern Economic Review*,

27 May 1993, p. 14.

[32] *Wen Wei Po* (Hong Kong), 7 December 1991, in FBIS-CHI-91-243, 18 December 1991, pp. 10–11, *South China Morning Post*, 31 December 1992, p. 8, *Financial Times*, 9 July 1993.

[33] *Zhongguo Xinwen She*, 11 June 1993, in *FE/1738/B2/4*, and the same agency on 6 July in *FE/1746/B2/3*. See also *Far Eastern Economic Review*, 3 June 1993, pp. 26–27, and *Asia Inc*, November 1993, pp. 37–47.

[34] *Zhongguo Tongxun She*, 25 October 1993, in *FE/1834/G/1*.

[35] *IHT*, 10 June 1993, and *The Economist*, 10 July 1993.

[36] *The Economist*, 24 April 1993.

[37] Gerald Segal, 'The Coming Confrontation Between China and Japan', *World Policy Journal*, Summer 1993.

[38] *Financial Times*, 1 June 1993.

[39] *The Economist*, 21 August 1993.

[40] *Xinhua*, 2 September 1992, in FBIS-CHI-92-171, 2 September 1992, p. 11, and *Xinhua*, 24 August 1993, in *FE/ 0300/WG/3*.

[41] Yao Jianguo, 'A Dynamic Bohai Rim Looms on the Horizon', *Beijing Review*, 13–19 December 1993, and *Asian Wall Street Journal*, 7 December 1993.

[42] On the regional pattern, see Gerald Segal, *The Soviet Union and the Pacific* (Boston, MA: Unwin/Hyman for the RIIA, 1990), especially chapter 6. For recent data, see Mayak Radio, 15 August 1993, in SU/WO296/A/8-9.

[43] *Xinhua*, 29 August 1993, in *FE/0298/ WG/6*.

[44] *Liaowang* (Hong Kong), no. 40, 5 October 1992, in FBIS-CHI-92-211, 30 October, pp. 21–23, *Christian Science Monitor*, 14 August 1992; *Financial Times*, 23 February 1992; *Far Eastern Economic Review*, 8 July 1993, pp. 40–43, 21 October 1993, pp. 20–21, and *Zhongguo Xinwen She*, 11 December 1993, in *FE/1871/G/5*.

[45] Despite wilder stories, these are the

only confirmed deals as reported by Russia to the United Nations Arms Register. See *Moscow News*, no. 29, 16 July 1993, p. 5.

[46] ITAR-TASS, 3 June 1993, in SU/1707/A1/5, ITAR-TASS, 19 June, in *FE*/1734/A1/5, *Postfactum*, 6 July 1993, in SU/1740/A1/1-2, ITAR-TASS, 9 July 1993, in SU/1737/i, and Ostankino Channel 1 TV, 4 July 1993, in SU/1733/A1/5. Mayak Radio, 10 September 1993, in *FE*/1794/G/2.

[47] *Kommersant*, Moscow, 17 April 1993, in SU/1676/A1/3-4, and *Krasnaya Zvezda*, 7 May 1993, reporting that some disputes had become 'an acute issue', SU/1689/A1/1. See also Pi Ying-hsien, 'China's Boundary Issues with the former Soviet Union', *Issues and Studies*, July 1992.

[48] *South China Morning Post*, 28 June 1993, and *Far Eastern Economic Review*, 17 June 1993, p. 52.

[49] Lillian Craig Harris, 'Xinjiang, Central Asia and the Implication for China's Policy in the Islamic World', and Gaye Christoffersen, 'Xinjiang and the Great Islamic Circle', *The China Quarterly*, no. 133, March 1993.

[50] *KazTag*, 9 July 1993, in SU/1739/A1/4-5.

[51] Roland Dannreuther, *Creating New States in Central Asia*, Adelphi Paper 288 (London: Brassey's for the IISS, 1994), and Radio Moscow, 6 September 1993, in SU/1791/G/1.

[52] *Xinhua*, 30 April 1993, in SU/W0280/A7, and *Xinhua*, 29 May 1993, in *FE*/W0286/A7. See also an interview with Nazarbayev on Ostankino Channel 1 TV, Moscow, in SU/1845/G/1-2.

[53] *Xinhua*, 24 July 1992, in FBIS-CHI-92-147, 30 July 1992, pp. 60–61, *Xinhua*, 2 August 1992, in FBIS-CHI-92-151, 5 August 1992, pp. 62–63, and *Xinhua*, 21 March 1993, in FBIS-CHI-93-054, 23 March 1993, p. 9. See also J. Richard Walsh, 'China and the New Geopolitics of Central Asia', *Asian Survey*, no. 3, March 1993.

[54] *Daily Telegraph*, 4 January 1994, reporting details of Prime Minister Bhutto's trip to China in December.

[55] Kazakh TV, 5 October 1993, in SU/1817/G1-5, and various reports on his visit to China in October 1993 in SU/1824/G/1-2. *The Washington Post*, 6 May 1992. See also Nazarbayev's interview, 10 November, Ostankino Channel 1 TV, in SU/1845/G/1-2.

[56] Dannreuther, *Central Asia*.

Chapter III

[1] See various articles, but especially Yan Jiaqi on federalism, *China Now*, no. 143, Winter 1992–93.

[2] Waldron, 'Warlordism Versus Federalism'.